INVESTING IN RENTAL PROPERTIES FOR BEGINNERS

The Financial Anxiety Solution

By

John Kingov

Investing in Rental Properties for Beginners

The Financial Anxiety Solution

Copyright Note

investments. The properties we're talking about range from $30,000 to $50,000, located in middle-class neighborhoods across the country. These are not luxury condos or beachfront homes, but they're safe, affordable, and—most importantly—they make a real difference.

The homes we'll discuss offer an unprecedented opportunity to build wealth while giving back. They provide a chance to inject capital, life, and prosperity into areas that have been overlooked for too long. And guess what? They're not just beneficial for the community; these investments are also profitable. We're talking about high returns and a steady cash flow—the kind of financial stability you can't always find in the stock market or other volatile investment avenues.

This book is not just about investing; it's about making an impact. It's about reclaiming the narrative and understanding that wealth is not just about where we put our money, but how we use it to shape our world. It's about leveraging the opportunity in the overlooked, the underappreciated, the low-priced neighborhoods, and transforming them into vibrant communities while securing a financial future for ourselves.

So, if you're ready to dive into a world of investment that is as rewarding socially as it is financially, I invite you to turn the page. Let's embark on this journey to reclaim our wealth and reshape our neighborhoods together.

You might have a few questions about the person guiding you through this adventure. Who am I? Why have I chosen this unconventional path to wealth? Let me introduce myself formally: I'm Lisa Phillips, an ordinary woman with an extraordinary passion for helping people like you unearth the opportunities in the often-ignored, low-cost real estate market.

Before I found my footing in the realm of real estate, I was not much different from many of you reading this book. I was not born into wealth, and the real estate market seemed like an intimidating venture. But through resilience, research, and a bit of trial and error, I found a niche that not only promised financial returns but also echoed my desire to make a positive societal impact. Over time, I have managed to aid thousands of investors in securing their financial future by investing in properties priced between $30,000 to

$50,000 in middle-class neighborhoods all over the nation.

Investing locally or out-of-state, regardless of geographical barriers, has become my calling. I've discovered that helping professionals gain access to real estate investing in a price range they can afford is more than just a career—it's an avenue for change. A way to alter not just their own financial circumstances, but also to contribute to the upliftment of the communities they invest in.

This book is designed to be a practical, hands-on guide that will provide you with the tools and insights needed to navigate the world of low-cost property investment successfully. You won't need to knock on the doors of banks or plead with friends or family for loans. Instead, you will learn how to build a profitable rental portfolio by purchasing units in modest neighborhoods that offer impressive rent returns. Think of buying a $44,000 rental that brings in $1200 a month in rent—that's the kind of potential we're tapping into.

The aim of this book is not just to equip you with the knowledge needed to start your journey in real estate investment but to instill the confidence and insight needed to tread this path successfully. By the end of this book, you should have a comprehensive understanding of the low-cost real estate investment landscape and the tools needed to make your mark in it.

So, are you ready to convert your dreams of becoming a real estate investor into a reality? Are you prepared to achieve financial freedom and make a positive impact on your community? If your answer is a resounding 'yes,' then this journey is for you. Turn the page, and let's get started on this exciting journey together.

Chapter 1

Understanding Real Estate Investing

Explaining Passive Income and Generational Wealth

Before we dive into the nuts and bolts of real estate investing, it's essential to understand some fundamental concepts that lie at the heart of this endeavor: passive income and generational wealth. Understanding these concepts will not only give you a clearer picture of why real estate investing is such an attractive prospect, but it will also fuel your motivation as you navigate this path.

Passive Income

In its simplest terms, passive income refers to money earned on a regular basis with minimal or no effort to maintain it. It's the dream of many, from working professionals tired of the 9-to-5 grind to retirees seeking to supplement their pensions. Passive income provides a financial safety net that can grow over time without proportionate increases in effort or time.

In the world of real estate, passive income typically comes from rental properties. Once you've invested in a property and found reliable tenants, you'll start receiving rental income. Of course, there will be some maintenance costs and potential vacancies, but a well-managed property can provide consistent, reliable income.

Generational Wealth

Generational wealth, on the other hand, is wealth that is passed down from one generation to the next. This could be in the form of money, real estate, stocks, or a family business. The key feature of generational wealth is that it provides financial security for future generations.

In our context, buying a rental property isn't just about earning money in the present day—it's also about securing a financial asset that can benefit your family for years, even decades, to come. If managed properly, a real estate property can continue to generate income or appreciate in value, becoming a potent tool for building generational wealth.

The beauty of investing in real estate lies in the intersection of these two concepts. With a single investment, you can create a source of passive income for yourself and also build generational wealth to secure your family's future. The idea of creating a stable, recurring income stream and a long-lasting financial legacy is what draws many to real estate investing, and for a good reason.

Now that we understand these key motivators let's delve deeper into the specifics of real estate investing and how we can use it to achieve these financial goals.

A Brief History and Overview of Real Estate Market Changes

To appreciate where we are and where we might be going in the world of real estate investing, it helps to understand the history of the market and how it has evolved over time.

The world of real estate has a rich and complex history, tracing back centuries. However, the modern era of real estate investing as we understand it began to take shape in the 20th century. It was in the 1950s and 1960s that the real estate market began to emerge as an attractive investment opportunity for the average individual. It became more common for families to own their homes, and the concept of buying additional properties as an investment started to become a reality.

In the 1970s and 1980s, inflation rates soared, and many investors turned to real estate as a shield against inflation. During these times, property values and rental rates increased, and real estate proved to be a good investment.

The late 1990s and early 2000s saw a boom in the housing market, fuelled in part by low interest rates and looser lending standards. However, this led to the real estate bubble and subsequent crash in 2007-2008, causing one of the most significant recessions in history.

Since the Great Recession, the real estate market has rebounded. Interest rates have remained low, and while lending standards have tightened, many investors have found real estate to be a reliable investment avenue. Today, real estate stands strong as an asset class that can provide good returns, and it's considered a key part of a diversified investment portfolio.

However, it's important to note that the real estate market isn't uniform—it's made up of numerous local markets, each with its own dynamics and trends. This is where our focus on low-cost neighborhoods comes into play. While high-end real estate in major cities may grab headlines, there's a lot of potentials in more affordable areas. These markets can often offer good returns and have the additional benefit of being more accessible to beginner investors.

In the upcoming sections, we'll delve into the nuances of the real estate market and provide a guide on how to navigate it successfully, particularly focusing on these affordable investment opportunities. The goal is to equip you with the knowledge and tools to find and seize opportunities, no matter where they might be.

The Comparison Between Real Estate and Other Forms of Investments Like the Stock Market

As we delve deeper into the world of real estate investing, it's crucial to understand how it stacks up against other investment options, most notably, the stock market. Both have their unique features, benefits, and drawbacks, and understanding these can help you make informed decisions about where to put your money.

Stability

One of the biggest draws of real estate is its relative stability compared to the stock market. While property values can and do fluctuate, they tend to do so much more gradually than stock prices. The stock market is highly sensitive to a plethora of factors—everything from geopolitical events to corporate earnings reports can send stock prices soaring or plummeting within hours. Real estate, on the other hand, isn't as directly affected by such factors, making it a less volatile investment.

Tangible Asset

Real estate is a tangible asset—you can see it, touch it, and utilize it. This tangible nature of real estate provides a sense of security that intangible investments like stocks cannot offer. In addition, owning a physical property means you can leverage it in ways that are not possible with stocks—for instance, by renting it out to generate income or using it as collateral for a loan.

Income Generation

Both real estate and stocks have the potential to provide investors with a regular income stream—rental income in the case of real estate, and dividends in the case of stocks. However, not all stocks pay dividends, and those that do can stop or reduce their payments without warning. In contrast, a well-chosen rental property can provide a consistent and even increasing income over time.

Control

When you buy a property, you have control over most aspects of your investment. You can choose the property, decide on the rent, select your tenants, and even influence the property's value by making improvements. With stocks, you're one of many shareholders and have little to no influence over the company's performance.

Leverage

Real estate allows for considerable leverage—you can buy a property worth $100,000 by paying a down payment of $20,000 and borrowing the rest. If the property appreciates in value, the return is based on the total value of the property, not just your initial down payment. While you can also buy stocks on margin, the ability to leverage is generally less than with real estate and comes with its own risks.

Tax Benefits

Real estate investing offers numerous tax advantages that aren't available to stock investors. These include the ability to deduct mortgage interest and property taxes, depreciation, and the possibility to defer capital gains tax through strategies like a 1031 exchange.

However, it's important to note that both forms of investment come with risks and should be approached thoughtfully. Real estate requires more hands-on management than stocks and can be less liquid in a pinch. Meanwhile, stocks can offer higher liquidity and sometimes impressive returns, but they can also be more volatile.

In the end, many successful investors choose to include both real estate and stocks in their portfolio, striking a balance that suits their individual goals, risk tolerance, and investment style. In the following chapters, we'll delve into how you can make the most of the unique benefits of real estate investing, particularly focusing on affordable rental properties.

Chapter 2

Low-Cost Real Estate: The Untapped Goldmine

Advantages of Investing in $30,000 to $50,000 Properties

As we embark on this exploration into the realms of affordable real estate investment, it's essential to understand why investing in properties in the $30,000 to $50,000 range can be such an appealing prospect. This might seem counter-intuitive—after all, in a society where success is often measured by the magnitude of one's assets, the notion of seeking wealth in the realm of the modest can seem contradictory. But as we'll see, the reality of investing in low-cost real estate uncovers a series of advantages that can make these properties a veritable goldmine for the discerning investor.

1. Accessibility

The first and perhaps most glaring advantage of low-cost real estate investment is its accessibility. For many would-be investors, the prospect of buying a property worth several hundred thousand dollars—or more—is simply out of reach. A significant number of people interested in investing in real estate often delay their plans, believing they need to save a substantial amount for a down payment. But by focusing on properties within the $30,000 to $50,000 range, the barrier to entry is substantially lowered. This opens up the real estate market to individuals who might otherwise have been excluded, and provides an accessible starting point for new investors.

2. Cash Flow

Properties in the $30,000 to $50,000 range can often generate surprisingly high rental income relative to their cost. It's entirely feasible, for example, to purchase a $40,000 property that rents for $800 per month. That equates to $9,600 per year—a return on investment of 24% before expenses. Even after accounting for costs like property management, maintenance, insurance, and taxes, the net return can still be significantly higher than what you might expect from a more expensive property or other types of investments.

3. Lower Risk

Investing in low-cost properties inherently carries less financial risk simply because less money is at stake. If you're investing in a $40,000 property and the market takes a downturn, you stand to lose far less than if you'd invested in a property worth hundreds of thousands of dollars. Additionally, because these properties are more affordable, it's possible to diversify by investing in multiple properties rather than putting all your eggs in one basket, further reducing your risk.

4. High Demand

Properties in the lower price range are typically located in working-class neighborhoods, which can be a significant advantage. There is always a high demand for affordable housing, making it easier to find tenants and maintain a steady rental income. In times of economic uncertainty, high-end rental markets may experience drops in demand, but the market for affordable rental units often remains robust.

5. Potential for Appreciation

While the primary focus of investing in low-cost rental properties is cash flow, there's also potential for property value appreciation. If you invest in up-and-coming neighborhoods or areas poised for growth, your property's value could increase over time. Even modest appreciation on a percentage basis can represent a significant return on your investment given the low initial purchase price.

6. Opportunity for Positive Impact

Last but certainly not least, investing in low-cost properties often means investing in neighborhoods that have been overlooked or underserved. As property owners, investors have the power to contribute positively to these communities. By maintaining and improving properties, you can contribute to neighborhood revitalization, provide quality housing, and even help to stabilize the community.

In conclusion, investing in properties in the $30,000 to $50,000 range offers a unique blend of accessibility, strong potential returns, lower risk, and the opportunity to make a positive impact. These factors make this an attractive and potentially lucrative niche in the real estate market that's worth exploring for both new and seasoned investors. In the following sections, we'll delve into the practical aspects of finding, buying, and managing these affordable investment properties, and how to navigate potential challenges to achieve success in this exciting venture.

Case Studies of Successful Investments in These Properties

Let's explore real-life examples to illustrate how investing in low-cost properties can yield promising results. These case studies show that with strategic planning, careful selection, and diligent management, you can find success in affordable real estate.

Case Study 1: The Out-of-State Investor

Meet John, a 30-year-old software engineer living in San Francisco. He was keen to start investing in real estate, but the sky-high property prices in his local market were out of his reach. Determined not to let geographical constraints limit him, John decided to look for affordable investment opportunities out of state.

After extensive research, he found a well-maintained, tenant-occupied duplex in a stable neighborhood in Cleveland, Ohio. The property was listed for $45,000, a price at which it was already generating a rental income of $950 per month.

John moved forward with the purchase, using a reputable local property management company to handle the day-to-day operations. Even after accounting for property management fees, maintenance reserves, property taxes, and insurance, he was able to net around $500 per month—over 13% return on his investment annually. The property also appreciated in value by about 3% per year, adding to his return on investment.

Case Study 2: The Local Investor

Next, let's look at Mary, a school teacher from Birmingham, Alabama. Mary had saved $35,000 over several years and was looking for a way to supplement her income. She decided to invest in a local property: a single-family home in a working-class neighborhood in her city. The property was listed for $30,000 and was already rented for $650 per month.

Mary bought the property and decided to manage it herself. After setting aside money for potential repairs and other expenses, she was still able to net around $400 per month. That's a 16% return on her investment from rental income alone. On top of that, the property appreciated at a rate of about 2% per year.

Case Study 3: The Portfolio Builder

Finally, let's consider the story of Robert, a retired police officer from Phoenix, Arizona. Robert had been a real estate investor for several years, focusing primarily on properties in the $30,000 to $50,000 range.

Over a period of 10 years, he had built a portfolio of 10 rental properties in various cities across the Midwest. Each property cost him between $30,000 and $50,000, and they collectively brought in around $8,500 per month in rental income.

Robert hired a property management company to handle day-to-day operations, and even after expenses, he netted around $4,000 per month. This income stream provided him with a comfortable retirement and the peace of mind that his investments were also growing in value over time.

These case studies illustrate the potential of investing in low-cost properties. Whether you're looking to buy a single property or build a portfolio, whether you're investing locally or out-of-state, there are opportunities out there that can provide a good return on investment and a significant income stream.

In the next chapter, we'll provide guidance on how to find these investment opportunities and the factors to consider when choosing a property. We'll also discuss strategies for financing these investments and how to manage your properties to ensure a steady stream of rental income.

The Potential for Positive Community Impact

One of the most rewarding aspects of investing in low-cost properties in middle-class neighborhoods is the potential to positively impact the communities where these properties are located. When done responsibly, investing in these neighborhoods can promote stability, contribute to the local economy, and even foster a sense of community pride. Let's delve into some of the ways real estate investors can make a positive difference.

1. Revitalizing Neighborhoods

Investing in real estate isn't just about purchasing a property; it's also about maintaining and improving it. When you invest in a property, you often spend money on renovations, landscaping, and regular upkeep. These improvements can enhance the neighborhood's overall aesthetics, fostering a sense of pride among residents and potentially encouraging other property owners to invest in their properties as well.

Take the case of Sarah, an investor who bought a run-down duplex in a struggling neighborhood in Pittsburgh for $40,000. She spent another $10,000 on renovations, transforming the dilapidated building into a beautiful and safe place to live. Not only did this improve the lives of her tenants, but it also had a ripple effect on the neighborhood. Other homeowners started improving their properties, and the whole block began to look better and feel safer.

2. Providing Quality Housing

There is a dire need for affordable, quality housing in many parts of the country. By investing in low-cost properties and maintaining them well, you can provide quality homes for individuals and families who might otherwise struggle to find decent housing within their budget.

Consider the example of David, who bought several low-cost properties in a working-class neighborhood in Indianapolis. He made sure all his properties were well-maintained and responded quickly to tenant concerns. As a result, he was able to provide affordable, quality housing for several families, improving their quality of life and earning their lasting appreciation.

3. Boosting Local Economies

Investing in real estate also has the potential to boost local economies. Money spent on property improvements often goes to local businesses and workers. Furthermore, tenants living in your properties will likely spend money in their local community, supporting local businesses.

For instance, when Lisa, an investor from Atlanta, bought a handful of properties in a low-cost neighborhood, she hired local contractors for all the necessary renovation work. She also made it a point to purchase supplies from local stores. As a result, her investments contributed to the local economy, supporting jobs and businesses in the community.

4. Encouraging Community Stability

By providing quality, affordable housing, real estate investors can also promote stability in the communities where they invest. Stable, long-term tenants are more likely to take an active interest in their community, engaging in local activities, sending their children to local schools, and generally contributing to a vibrant community.

When Tom invested in several properties in a low-cost neighborhood in Memphis, he made an effort to select reliable, long-term tenants. Over time, his tenants became pillars of the community, organizing neighborhood watch programs, participating in local events, and contributing to a strong, supportive community atmosphere.

The potential for making a positive community impact is one of the most gratifying aspects of investing in low-cost properties. Not only does this approach to investing offer significant financial rewards, but it also provides the opportunity to make a real, tangible difference in people's lives and communities. This blend of financial and social returns makes investing in these properties a truly fulfilling endeavor.

As we continue in the next chapters, we'll explore how you can prepare for and succeed in your real estate investment journey, how to select and finance your properties, and how to manage them for maximum financial and community benefit. Whether you're a first-time investor or looking to expand your portfolio, the opportunities and rewards in low-cost real estate investing await.

Chapter 3

Preparing to Invest: Financial Planning

Financial Considerations and Planning

Before taking your first step into the realm of real estate investing, it's critical to lay a solid financial foundation. While investing in $30,000 to $50,000 properties is more affordable than many other real estate ventures, it's still a significant commitment that requires careful planning and preparation. Here, we'll explore some of the crucial financial considerations and how to prepare yourself for this exciting journey.

1. Assessing Your Financial Situation

The first step is to take an honest look at your current financial situation. This includes your income, savings, expenses, and any debts you may have. You should have a clear understanding of how much you can afford to invest without jeopardizing your financial stability or lifestyle.

Consider the case of Alice, a young professional looking to get started in real estate investing. Before she bought her first property, Alice sat down and took a hard look at her finances. She factored in her monthly income, her regular expenses, and her existing student loan debt. She also evaluated her savings to determine what she could comfortably afford as a down payment and potential property improvement costs.

2. Building an Emergency Fund

Next, it's vital to have an emergency fund in place before you start investing. This is a fund that can cover your living expenses for at least 3-6 months. It acts as a financial safety net, protecting you in case of unexpected events like job loss, health issues, or significant repairs on your rental property.

Consider John, who had built up an emergency fund of six months' worth of expenses before he started investing in real estate. When a major system in one of his rental properties unexpectedly needed replacement, he was able to cover the cost from his emergency fund without disrupting his cash flow or dipping into his personal savings.

3. Understanding Cash Flow and Return on Investment (ROI)

One of the most critical financial considerations when investing in real estate is understanding cash flow and return on investment. Cash flow is the money that you'll be left with each month after all expenses, including mortgage payments, property management, taxes, insurance, and maintenance.

Return on investment, on the other hand, is a measure of the profitability of your investment. It's calculated by dividing the annual return (cash flow plus any appreciation in property value) by the total amount of money you've invested.

As an investor, your aim should be to find properties that will provide positive cash flow and a good return on investment. For example, Lisa bought a property for $40,000 and spent an additional $5,000 on renovations. She rents it out for $800 a month. After paying all her expenses, she nets $400 a month, which equates to $4,800 a year. Her total investment in the property is $45,000, so her return on investment is approximately 10.67%.

4. Preparing for the Unexpected

It's also important to budget for unexpected expenses. These can include major repairs, vacancies between tenants, or sudden changes in the property market. A good rule of thumb is to set aside 5-10% of your rental income for these unexpected costs.

5. Financing Your Investment

Finally, you'll need to think about how you'll finance your investment. Most people don't have the cash to buy a property outright, so financing will likely be part of your investment strategy. This can include traditional mortgages, home equity loans, or even partnering with other investors.

For instance, Mark didn't have enough savings to buy a property outright. But he had a good credit score and a steady income, so he was able to secure a mortgage with a favorable interest rate. He used his savings for the down payment and renovation costs and financed the rest with his mortgage.

To wrap up, before you dive into real estate investing, it's crucial to have a strong financial plan in place. By assessing your financial situation, building an emergency fund, understanding cash flow and ROI, preparing for unexpected costs, and arranging your financing, you can set yourself up for success in your real estate investment journey. In the following sections, we'll delve deeper into the process of finding, analyzing, and buying your first property.

Tailoring Your Investment Strategy to Your Budget

Every successful real estate investor knows that one size does not fit all when it comes to investment strategies. Your budget plays a crucial role in determining your approach to real estate investing. Let's explore how you can tailor your investment strategy to fit your budget and meet your financial goals.

1. Setting Clear Financial Goals

The first step in tailoring your investment strategy to your budget is to set clear financial goals. What are you hoping to achieve through real estate investing? Are you seeking a supplemental income stream, planning for retirement, or looking to replace your full-time job? The answers to these questions will guide your investment strategy and help you determine what kind of property you can afford and what kind of return you'll need.

For example, Emily, a full-time teacher, was looking for a way to supplement her income. She didn't have a lot of money saved up, but she had a steady income and good credit. Her goal was to generate an extra $500 per month in cash flow. Knowing this, she tailored her strategy to look for properties in the $30,000 to $50,000 range that could meet this cash flow goal after expenses.

2. Investing Within Your Means

The cornerstone of a budget-tailored investment strategy is to invest within your means. It's essential to stick to a budget that allows you to maintain a comfortable lifestyle and doesn't stretch your finances too thin.

If you're new to real estate investing, the $30,000 to $50,000 range can be a good starting point as it requires less initial capital and can still generate a solid return. You don't have to go into substantial debt or deplete your life savings to get started in real estate investing. By staying within your budget, you can invest responsibly while building wealth over time.

3. Taking Advantage of Creative Financing Options

If your budget is limited, that doesn't necessarily mean you're priced out of the real estate market. There are numerous creative financing options you can explore. These might include seller financing, partnerships, private money loans, or leveraging a home equity line of credit. However, it's important to understand that each of these options comes with its own risks and benefits. Be sure to do your homework and consult with a financial advisor or experienced real estate investor before pursuing these options.

Consider Paul, who had a modest amount of savings but also had a lot of equity in his primary residence. He was able to use a home equity line of credit to finance his first rental property purchase, thereby leveraging his existing assets to grow his real estate portfolio.

4. Diversifying Your Investment Portfolio

Even within the realm of low-cost real estate, there's room for diversification. This can mean buying properties in different neighborhoods, cities, or even states. It might also mean diversifying the types of properties you invest in, such as single-family homes, duplexes, or condos. Diversifying your portfolio can help spread risk and increase your chances of steady returns.

For instance, Sarah, an investor with a limited budget, decided to diversify her portfolio by purchasing two properties in different states—one in Indiana and another in Tennessee. This diversification gave her two different rental markets to tap into, thereby spreading her risk and potential for income.

5. Continually Educating Yourself

The real estate market is dynamic and constantly changing. It's crucial to keep educating yourself and staying updated on market trends, investment strategies, financing options, and more. The more knowledge you have, the better equipped you'll be to tailor your investment strategy to your budget and maximize your returns.

In conclusion, tailoring your investment strategy to your

budget is a crucial aspect of successful real estate investing. It involves setting clear financial goals, investing within your means, taking advantage of creative financing options, diversifying your investment portfolio, and continually educating yourself. By following these guidelines, you can build a profitable real estate investment portfolio that fits within your budget and helps you achieve your financial goals. In the upcoming sections, we'll dive deeper into how to find and analyze potential investment properties within your budget range.

The Concept of Investing Without Loans

The traditional route to real estate investing often involves taking out a loan or mortgage to finance a property purchase. However, it's not the only way, and for some investors, the idea of buying properties without loans might be more appealing. This strategy can minimize risk, increase cash flow, and give you greater control over your investments. Let's delve into the concept of investing without loans and how you can apply this strategy in your own real estate investment journey.

1. The Appeal of Debt-Free Investing

The primary appeal of investing without loans is the reduction of risk. When you take out a loan, you're committing to regular payments over a long period, and if for any reason you can't make those payments, you risk losing your property. On the other hand, if you own a property outright, you're not beholden to any lender, and you have much more flexibility in managing your investment.

Furthermore, investing without loans can dramatically increase your cash flow. Without a mortgage payment to make every month, all of your rental income—after other expenses—goes straight into your pocket. This can result in a higher return on investment and more cash on hand for emergencies, property improvements, or future investments.

2. Strategies for Investing Without Loans

So how can you invest in real estate without taking out loans? Here are a few strategies:

Saving and Investing: The most straightforward way is to save up enough money to buy a property outright. While this can take time, investing in affordable properties in the

$30,000 to $50,000 range makes this a feasible goal for many people. And while you're saving, the money can be invested in low-risk assets that provide a modest return and can be easily liquidated when you're ready to buy.

Seller Financing: In some cases, the seller of a property may be willing to finance the purchase. This means you make your payments to the seller instead of a bank. Seller financing can offer more flexible terms than traditional loans, and you might be able to negotiate a lower down payment, a lower interest rate, or a longer repayment period.

Partnerships: Another option is to partner with someone else to buy a property. This could be a friend, family member, or business partner. The key here is to have a clear agreement on who is responsible for what and what happens to the property if one partner wants out.

Real Estate Crowdfunding: Real estate crowdfunding platforms allow you to invest in real estate with a relatively small amount of money. You pool your money with other investors to buy a property or a share in a property. This can be a way to invest in real estate without taking on debt, although it also means you don't have full control over the property.

3. Balancing Risk and Reward

Investing in real estate without loans is not without risks. It ties up a lot of your capital in one place, and if the property loses value or if something happens that prevents you from renting it out, you could lose money. It's essential to carefully consider the potential risks and rewards, and to diversify your investments to protect yourself.

4. Harnessing the Power of Cash

There's a saying in real estate that "cash is king," and it applies here too. When you can afford to buy a property outright, you're in a stronger position to negotiate a lower price. Sellers are often willing to accept a lower offer from a buyer who can pay in cash and close quickly, rather than waiting for another buyer to secure financing.

In conclusion, investing without loans is a viable strategy that can offer numerous benefits, including reduced risk, increased cash flow, and greater control over your investments. By understanding and utilizing the various strategies for investing without loans, and balancing risk and reward carefully, you can successfully grow your real estate portfolio and financial wealth. In the next sections, we'll explore the process of finding and analyzing potential investment properties, how to make an offer and close the deal, and how to effectively manage your properties for maximum returns.

Chapter 4

Finding and Financing Your Property

Finding the Perfect Entry Points

The success of your real estate investment journey begins with finding the right property at the right price. But how do you find these perfect entry points? This requires a combination of research, patience, and sometimes thinking outside the box. Let's dive into how you can identify and capitalize on the best entry points in your real estate investing journey.

1. Understanding Market Cycles

Every real estate market goes through cycles, which

typically include periods of increasing property values, times when values peak, periods when prices decline, and times when the market stabilizes. These cycles are influenced by a variety of factors, including economic conditions, interest rates, and demographic trends.

Investors who understand these cycles can take advantage of them by buying properties when prices are low, such as during a market slowdown or a period of decline. It's important to remember that real estate is a long-term investment, and temporary market downturns can provide excellent opportunities to buy properties at a discount.

2. Identifying Undervalued Markets

One of the most effective strategies for finding the perfect entry points is to look for undervalued markets. These are areas where property prices are low compared to the rental income they can generate, or where prices haven't yet caught up with the area's growth or potential.

These markets can often be found in second-tier cities or suburban areas that are experiencing population growth, infrastructure development, or other positive changes. For example, a city might be attracting new businesses that bring jobs, or a new transit line might be making a suburban area more accessible and desirable.

3. Building a Local Team

Having a team on the ground in your chosen market is invaluable. This could include real estate agents, property managers, contractors, and other investors. These professionals understand the local market and can help you identify opportunities that others might miss.

For instance, when Sam, an investor from New York, decided to invest in properties in Ohio, he first built a team of local professionals. His real estate agent knew the local market inside and out and was able to guide him to neighborhoods that were undervalued but on the rise. His property manager was able to give him insights into the rental market, and his contractor helped him accurately estimate repair costs.

4. Using Online Resources

There are numerous online resources that can help you find potential investment properties. These include real estate listing sites, online marketplaces for investors, and property data platforms that provide information on property values, rental rates, market trends, and more.

However, it's important to remember that while these tools can provide valuable insights, they should not replace your own research and analysis. Always verify the information you find online and consult with local real estate professionals.

5. Networking with Other Investors

Joining real estate investment clubs or online forums can be a great way to find potential investment properties. Other investors can share their experiences, provide tips on markets or neighborhoods to consider, and even offer specific property leads. Just remember to do your own due diligence on any potential investments.

6. Considering Off-Market Properties

Off-market properties, or properties that are not publicly listed for sale, can often be purchased at lower prices than comparable listed properties. These might include foreclosures, short sales, or properties owned by individuals who need to sell quickly. Finding these opportunities often requires networking, direct outreach, or working with a real estate agent who specializes in off-market properties.

In conclusion, finding the perfect entry points for your real estate investments involves understanding market cycles, identifying undervalued markets, building a local team, using online resources, networking with other investors, and considering off-market properties. By mastering these strategies, you can find properties that provide excellent value and potential for strong returns. In the next section, we will delve into the various financing options available to you and how to choose the right one for your investment strategy.

Creative Tips for Finding Incredible Deals

The ability to find great real estate deals can significantly impact the profitability of your investment. While browsing online listings and working with real estate agents are common ways of finding properties, there are also several more creative strategies that can help you uncover excellent investment opportunities. In this section, we'll explore some of these methods.

1. Networking

Never underestimate the power of a solid professional network. Building relationships with a wide range of individuals and professionals within the real estate industry can provide you with insider information and leads on potential deals. Attend local real estate investor meetups, join online real estate forums, and engage with other investors on social media platforms.

Don't limit your network to only other investors, though. Professionals such as real estate attorneys, accountants, property managers, and contractors often have their finger on the pulse of the local market and can be a source of valuable leads. Remember, networking is about building reciprocal relationships. Share your knowledge and leads, and others will likely do the same.

2. Direct Mail Marketing

While it might seem a bit old-fashioned in the digital age, direct mail marketing can be an effective way to find potential deals. This involves sending out letters or postcards to homeowners in your target market, indicating your interest in buying properties. You can get lists of homeowners from various sources, such as the local county recorder's office or online data providers.

While it's a numbers game and might require sending out a large volume of mail to get a few responses, the deals you do get are often worth the effort. Homeowners who respond are usually highly motivated to sell, allowing you to negotiate favorable purchase terms.

3. Driving for Dollars

Driving for dollars involves physically driving around neighborhoods to look for potential investment properties. You're primarily looking for signs of distressed properties, such as neglected landscaping, boarded-up windows, or notices posted on the door. Once you identify a potential property, you can use public records or a skip tracing service to find the owner's contact information and reach out to them directly.

This method can be time-consuming but is often effective in finding off-market deals. Moreover, it provides you with a deeper understanding of the neighborhoods in which you're investing.

4. Wholesalers

Working with wholesalers is another way to find great real estate deals. Wholesalers are investors who specialize in finding undervalued properties, putting them under contract, and then selling that contract to another investor.

While you typically pay more when buying from a wholesaler than you would if you found the deal yourself, it can save you time and effort. Just ensure you thoroughly vet the wholesaler and the deal to make sure you're still getting a good value.

5. Foreclosure and Auction Sales

Purchasing properties in foreclosure or at auction can provide significant discounts. When a homeowner fails to pay their mortgage, the lender may foreclose on the property. It's then often sold at a public auction.

Buying foreclosures or auction properties can be risky and often requires a significant amount of upfront cash. However, with thorough due diligence and careful bidding, it can result in excellent deals.

6. Online Marketplaces

There are numerous online marketplaces and platforms

specializing in investment properties. These platforms can connect you with off-market deals, foreclosures, short sales, and more.

Some of these platforms also provide property data and analytics, which can be valuable in evaluating potential deals. Remember, though, that you should always conduct your own due diligence before purchasing a property.

By using these creative strategies, you can uncover real estate deals that other investors might miss. This can give you a competitive advantage and increase the profitability of your investments. In the next section, we'll explore various financing options for your investment properties and how to choose the right one for you.

Different Financing Options and How to Secure Them

Securing financing is often one of the most challenging aspects of real estate investing, particularly for beginners. Fortunately, several financing options can suit a variety of circumstances and investment strategies. Let's delve into these options and discuss how you can secure them effectively.

1. Conventional Mortgage

A conventional mortgage is the most common type of financing used by real estate investors. These loans are offered by banks and other financial institutions and are typically used to purchase single-family homes or smaller multi-unit properties.

To secure a conventional mortgage, you will need a good credit score, a stable income, and a sufficient down payment (usually 20% for investment properties). You'll also need to demonstrate that the rental income from the property will cover the mortgage payments and other expenses.

2. FHA Loans

The Federal Housing Administration (FHA) offers loans that are particularly popular among first-time homebuyers and investors in small multi-family properties. With an FHA loan, you can put down as little as 3.5%.

However, to qualify for an FHA loan, you must plan to live in one of the units of the property for at least a year. This makes FHA loans an excellent option for those looking to get started in house hacking, a strategy where you live in one unit of a multi-family property and rent out the others.

3. Home Equity Loans and HELOCs

If you have substantial equity in your home, you can use a home equity loan or a home equity line of credit (HELOC) to finance an investment property purchase. A home equity loan gives you a lump sum of cash, which you repay over a set period. A HELOC works more like a credit card, where you have a line of credit you can draw from as needed.

These options can be easier to qualify for than other types of loans, as they're secured by your home. However, they also come with the risk that if you can't repay the loan, you could lose your home.

4. Private Money Lenders

Private money lenders are individuals or groups who lend money for real estate investments. These can be friends, family members, business associates, or professional private lenders.

Private money loans can offer more flexibility than traditional loans, both in terms of the loan terms and the types of properties you can purchase. However, they often come with higher interest rates. To secure private money, you'll need to demonstrate that your investment will be profitable and that you have a clear plan for repaying the loan.

5. Hard Money Lenders

Hard money lenders are professional lenders who specialize in short-term loans for real estate investments, often used for fix-and-flip projects. They focus more on the value of the property and its potential than your credit score.

Hard money loans can be expensive, with high interest rates and fees, but they're relatively easy to secure and can be processed quickly. You'll need a solid plan and a potentially profitable property to qualify.

6. Real Estate Crowdfunding

Real estate crowdfunding platforms connect investors with real estate projects that need funding. As an investor, you can contribute a small amount towards a project and earn a return based on the project's profits. It's a way to invest in real estate without the need to manage properties yourself.

Each crowdfunding platform has its own criteria for

investors, so be sure to understand these before investing.

In conclusion, there are many different financing options for real estate investments, and each has its pros and cons. It's essential to understand these, align them with your investment strategy, and make sure you're comfortable with the level of risk involved. Always conduct thorough due diligence and consider seeking advice from financial advisors or experienced investors. In the next chapter, we'll discuss the next steps after you've secured financing and found a potential investment property: making an offer and closing the deal.

Chapter 5

The Buying Process

How to Find Potential Properties

In the world of real estate investing, identifying potential properties is where the rubber meets the road. It's where all your preparation and planning start to take concrete form. Finding potential properties requires a combination of strategic thinking, thorough research, and a willingness to leave no stone unturned. Let's explore some of the key strategies and methods you can use to uncover potential investment properties.

1. Define Your Investment Criteria

The first step in finding potential properties is defining your investment criteria. This means determining what type of properties you're looking for based on your investment strategy, financial goals, and risk tolerance. Consider factors such as the type of property (single-family, multi-family, etc.), the location (urban, suburban, rural), the price range, and the potential for income (rental yield or resale value).

Your investment criteria will act as a filter, helping you sift through the vast array of available properties to identify those that align with your investment strategy. For instance, if you're focusing on properties in the $30,000 to $50,000 range in up-and-coming neighborhoods, you can discard properties that fall outside of this scope.

2. Leverage Online Resources

The internet has revolutionized how real estate investors find potential properties. Numerous websites and platforms allow you to search for properties based on your criteria. These include mainstream real estate websites like Zillow, Redfin, and Realtor.com, as well as platforms specifically for investors, such as LoopNet, Auction.com, and BiggerPockets.

In addition to listing properties for sale, many of these sites provide valuable data, such as property details, sales history, tax information, and more. This can help you in your initial assessment of a property's potential as an investment.

3. Work with a Local Real Estate Agent

A knowledgeable local real estate agent can be a valuable asset in your property search. They have an in-depth understanding of the local market, access to listings that may not be publicly available, and the ability to quickly assess properties based on your criteria.

When choosing an agent, look for someone who has experience working with investors and understands your investment strategy. Be clear about what you're looking for and communicate your criteria to them clearly.

4. Network with Other Investors and Industry Professionals

Networking with other real estate investors and industry professionals can lead to opportunities that you wouldn't find elsewhere. Investors often share information about potential deals, and professionals like property managers, contractors, and real estate attorneys can provide leads on properties that might be coming on the market soon.

Consider joining local real estate investment clubs, participating in online forums, and attending industry events. Always be ready to share what you're looking for, and be open to opportunities that come your way.

5. Explore Off-Market Opportunities

Don't limit your property search to properties that are currently for sale. Off-market properties, or properties that aren't officially listed, often present excellent investment opportunities. These can include foreclosures, properties owned by absentee owners, or properties owned by landlords who might be interested in selling.

Finding off-market properties often requires more legwork, including direct outreach to property owners, but can lead to deals with less competition and potentially better terms.

6. Drive for Dollars

Driving for dollars is a hands-on method that involves driving around targeted neighborhoods to identify potential properties. This strategy can be particularly effective in identifying distressed properties, which may not be listed for sale but whose owners may be motivated to sell. Signs of distressed properties might include noticeable disrepair, overgrown yards, or properties that appear vacant.

When you spot a potential property, take note of the address and then use public records, online tools, or a skip tracing service to find the property owner's contact details. Reach out to them directly to express your interest in buying the property.

7. Direct Mail Campaigns

Though it might seem somewhat old-fashioned, direct mail campaigns can be highly effective in generating leads for potential properties. This strategy involves sending out a large volume of letters or postcards to homeowners in your targeted area or demographic, expressing your interest in purchasing properties.

A well-executed direct mail campaign should be targeted, personalized, and followed up on. It can be time-consuming and requires some investment, but the results can be worth it. Owners who respond to direct mail are often highly motivated to sell, leading to some excellent buying opportunities.

8. Wholesale Deals

Wholesalers can be a valuable source of potential properties. These are individuals or companies who find and negotiate off-market deals, then sell the contract to an end buyer (like you) for a fee. Buying wholesale deals can save you time in finding and negotiating deals, but it's essential to do your due diligence to ensure you're getting a good deal.

In conclusion, finding potential properties is an active process that combines clear strategy, market knowledge, a bit of creativity, and sometimes, perseverance. While the strategies listed above can help you identify a wealth of opportunities, it's also essential to maintain focus and adhere to your investment criteria. Remember, the goal is not just to buy properties, but to buy properties that will contribute to your financial goals.

In the next section, we'll delve into the next crucial step in the buying process: analyzing potential properties to determine their viability as investments. This process will allow you to scrutinize each potential deal, assess its potential for return on investment, and identify any possible risks.

Making an Offer and Negotiating

Once you've found a potential investment property that meets your criteria, the next step is to make an offer and negotiate the terms of the sale. This is a critical stage in the buying process and requires a strategic approach to ensure you secure the property at the best possible price and terms. Let's explore this process in detail.

1. Conducting a Thorough Property Analysis

Before making an offer, it's essential to conduct a thorough analysis of the property. This involves assessing the condition of the property, estimating any necessary repair costs, analyzing the local market, and calculating the potential return on investment.

First, examine the property's condition. This may involve doing a walk-through yourself or hiring a professional inspector. You'll want to identify any potential issues, from structural problems to needed cosmetic updates. This will help you estimate the repair and renovation costs and factor them into your offer price.

Next, analyze the local market. This includes researching recent comparable sales (or "comps") in the area, understanding local rental rates, and evaluating the neighborhood's desirability and potential for appreciation. This will help you determine a fair offer price and estimate the property's potential for generating income and appreciation.

Finally, calculate the potential return on investment (ROI). This involves factoring in the purchase price, financing costs, repair and renovation costs, ongoing property management costs, and expected rental income. It's also wise to account for potential vacancies and maintenance issues. Your ROI should align with your investment goals and be competitive with other investment options available to you.

2. Determining Your Offer Price

Your offer price is one of the most critical parts of your offer. It's the number that will catch the seller's attention and form the basis for your negotiations. Your offer price should be based on your property analysis and aligned with your investment strategy.

Keep in mind that your initial offer doesn't need to be your highest price. In fact, it's often strategic to start lower to give yourself room to negotiate. However, your initial offer should still be realistic. An insultingly low offer can turn off sellers and hinder negotiations.

3. Structuring Your Offer

There's more to an offer than just the price. Other terms and conditions can influence how attractive your offer is to the seller. This might include your financing method, the amount of earnest money you're offering, your timeline for closing, any contingencies (such as a property inspection or financing contingency), and more.

Think about what's important to the seller. For example, if the seller is looking to close quickly, offering a fast closing timeline might make your offer more attractive. If the property is a fixer-upper, waiving certain repair requests might appeal to the seller.

Remember, everything is negotiable in real estate. Don't be afraid to get creative in structuring your offer to make it appealing to the seller.

4. Making Your Offer

Once you've determined your offer price and terms, the next step is to formally submit your offer. This is typically done in writing, often using a real estate purchase agreement form. In some cases, a simple letter of intent (LOI) may be used for the initial offer, with the formal purchase agreement completed once the main terms have been agreed upon.

It's generally a good idea to include a personal letter with your offer, particularly in a competitive market. A personal letter can help you stand out from other buyers and create an emotional connection with the seller. In the letter, you can explain why you want to buy the property and any plans you have for it.

5. Negotiating the Deal

After you've made your offer, the seller will review it and either accept it, reject it, or make a counteroffer. This is where your negotiation skills come into play.

Don't be discouraged if your initial offer isn't accepted. This is common in real estate transactions. Listen carefully to the seller's feedback or counteroffer and use it as a basis for negotiation. Remember, the goal is to arrive at a deal that meets your investment criteria and is acceptable to the seller.

If the seller makes a counteroffer, review it carefully. Consider how the revised price or terms align with your investment criteria and goals. If the counteroffer isn't acceptable, you can either make a new offer or walk away.

Negotiating a real estate deal can be a delicate process. It requires patience, diplomacy, and a willingness to compromise. Keep your emotions in check and make decisions based on your investment strategy and analysis, not on the heat of the moment.

6. Closing the Deal

Once you and the seller have agreed on the price and terms, the next step is to move towards closing. This involves finalizing the purchase agreement, satisfying any remaining contingencies (such as securing financing and conducting a property inspection), and preparing the necessary documents for the property transfer.

The closing process can be complex and involves various legal and financial details. It's generally recommended to work with a real estate attorney or a title company to ensure everything is done correctly.

7. Due Diligence

In real estate investing, due diligence refers to the process of verifying the information related to a property and the terms of its sale. This is a critical step that takes place before closing the deal, providing you, the buyer, with the opportunity to confirm that you're making a sound investment.

During the due diligence period, you should conduct a professional property inspection to identify any potential structural issues or necessary repairs that were not apparent during the initial viewing. This could include issues with the roof, plumbing, electrical systems, HVAC systems, or structural components of the building.

You should also review any legal aspects related to the property. This might include checking for any liens or encumbrances on the property, verifying that all property taxes are up to date, and ensuring that there are no legal issues that could affect your ownership of the property.

Due diligence also involves reviewing financial aspects of the property. For rental properties, this would involve verifying the current rent roll, reviewing leases, and understanding the overall profitability of the property.

If any issues arise during the due diligence process, you may have the option to renegotiate the purchase price, ask the seller to address the issue, or in some cases, back out of the deal completely.

8. The Art of Negotiation

Negotiation is a critical skill in real estate investing. The ability to negotiate effectively can be the difference between securing a good deal and overpaying for a property.

Successful negotiation involves a mix of preparation, clear

communication, and understanding the other party's needs and motivations. It's important to enter any negotiation with a clear idea of what you want, but also to be willing to compromise and find solutions that benefit both parties.

Remember, every aspect of a real estate transaction is negotiable - not just the price. This includes the terms of the deal, closing costs, and even what items are included in the sale.

Developing your negotiation skills can take time and practice. Consider reading books on negotiation, taking courses, or even practicing in everyday situations.

9. Securing Financing

After the offer has been accepted, and you've completed your due diligence, you'll need to finalize your financing. This process will vary depending on the type of financing you're using.

If you're using a conventional mortgage, this will involve working with your lender to complete the underwriting process. They'll verify your financial information, conduct a property appraisal, and prepare the loan for closing.

If you're using a private lender, hard money lender, or another non-traditional financing method, the process may be different. Make sure you understand what is required and stay in close communication with your lender to ensure everything progresses smoothly.

10. Closing on the Property

Closing is the final step in the buying process, where ownership of the property is officially transferred from the seller to the buyer. This involves signing a lot of paperwork, including the deed, the bill of sale, the affidavit of title, and the transfer tax declarations.

Upon closing, you'll also need to pay any closing costs. These can include loan origination fees, title insurance, property transfer taxes, and attorney fees.

After closing, the property is officially yours. Now, it's time to move on to managing the property and reaping the rewards of your investment. In the next section, we'll delve into the crucial aspects of property management, including finding and screening tenants, maintaining the property, and maximizing your rental income.

The Closing Process

Let's delve a bit deeper into the closing process now, also known as settlement, which is the final step in a real estate transaction. This process involves several essential steps, and understanding each one is crucial to ensure a smooth and successful closing.

1. Final Walkthrough

Before closing, conducting a final walkthrough of the property is advisable. This allows you to confirm that the property is in the same condition as when you made the offer, that any agreed-upon repairs have been completed, and that no new issues have arisen. If you identify any problems during the final walkthrough, you can address them before closing.

2. Closing Disclosure Review

Before the closing, your lender will provide a Closing Disclosure, a document that details the terms of your loan, your final closing costs, and any outstanding fees or charges. You should receive this document at least three days before closing, giving you enough time to review it and ask your lender any questions.

3. Closing Costs Payment

Closing costs include various fees associated with the real estate transaction, such as loan origination, appraisal, title insurance, and escrow fees. These costs typically amount to between 2% and 5% of the property's purchase price. Be prepared to pay these costs at closing.

4. Signing of Closing Documents

At the closing meeting, you'll sign various legal documents to finalize the property purchase. The number and type of documents can vary, but some key ones include:

The deed transfers ownership from the seller to you and contains information about the property and the people involved in the transaction.

The bill of sale confirms that the property, and any related personal property, is transferred.

The HUD-1 settlement statement outlines all costs related to the home sale.

The promissory note outlines the terms of the mortgage loan

and your promise to repay it.

Ensure you read and understand each document before signing. If there's anything you don't understand, ask your real estate agent, attorney, or lender for clarification.

5. Title Transfer and Recording

Once all documents have been signed and funds have been disbursed, the title to the property is officially transferred from the seller to you. The closing agent will then record the transaction in the county's public records, marking you as the new legal owner of the property.

6. Possession of the Property

After closing, you'll receive the keys to the property and can take possession. If it's a rental property, you'll also receive any security deposits and rent prorations from the seller.

In conclusion, while the closing process can be complex and may seem daunting, understanding each step can help you navigate it successfully. Remember, you have a team of professionals, including your real estate agent, attorney, and lender, to help guide you through the process. Once the closing process is complete, you're officially a real estate investor and ready to generate income from your new property. In the next chapter, we'll explore how to manage your rental property to maximize returns and build wealth over time.

Chapter 6

Owning and Managing Properties

How to Maintain Properties with Minimal Effort

One of the significant challenges of owning rental properties is maintenance. Keeping your property in good condition is essential for attracting and retaining quality tenants, preserving the value of your property, and ensuring you stay on the right side of housing regulations. However, property maintenance can also be time-consuming and expensive, particularly if it's not managed efficiently. In this section, we'll explore strategies to maintain your rental properties with minimal effort.

1. Regular Inspections and Preventive Maintenance

Prevention is better than cure, as the saying goes. This applies in the context of rental property maintenance too.

Regular inspections allow you to identify and fix small issues before they turn into major, costly repairs.

Set a schedule for property inspections—this could be once a year, twice a year, or even quarterly, depending on the age and condition of the property. During these inspections, check the property's overall condition and look for signs of potential issues, such as water leaks, structural damage, or pests.

Additionally, invest in preventive maintenance. This includes tasks such as servicing HVAC systems, cleaning gutters, and sealing cracks. Preventive maintenance might seem like an unnecessary expense, especially if everything seems to be working fine, but it can save you significant money and effort in the long run by extending the lifespan of your property's components and preventing major breakdowns.

2. Establish Good Relationships with Reliable Contractors

When you do need repairs or maintenance work done, having a reliable team of contractors can make the process much smoother and less stressful. This might include plumbers, electricians, handymen, HVAC technicians, and other specialists.

Start building your team of contractors as soon as you purchase your property. Get recommendations from other local landlords or real estate professionals, and try out different contractors for small jobs to see who does good work at a reasonable price.

Once you've found contractors you trust, nurture those relationships. Pay your bills promptly, communicate clearly and respectfully, and show appreciation for their work. Contractors who know and like you are more likely to go the extra mile for you, such as fitting you into their busy schedule when an emergency comes up.

3. Consider Hiring a Property Management Company

If you'd rather not deal with the day-to-day maintenance of your rental property, or if you're an out-of-state investor, hiring a property management company can be a good option. A property manager will handle all aspects of property maintenance, from routine inspections and preventive maintenance to arranging repairs and handling emergencies.

Property management companies do come at a cost—typically a percentage of the monthly rental income—but the cost can be worth it for the time and effort saved. If you choose to hire a property management company, do your due diligence to find a reputable company that offers good value for their fee.

4. Implement a System for Handling Maintenance Requests

Responding to maintenance requests in a timely and efficient manner is crucial for keeping your tenants happy and protecting your property. To do this, you'll need a system for handling maintenance requests.

This might involve using property management software that allows tenants to submit maintenance requests online, or it could be as simple as a dedicated phone number or email address for maintenance issues. Whatever system you choose, make sure your tenants know how to report maintenance issues and that you or your property manager respond to these requests promptly.

5. Set a Maintenance Budget

While it's crucial to keep your rental property in good

condition, it's equally important to do so in a cost-effective way. Setting a maintenance budget can help you manage your expenses and ensure that you're not overspending on upkeep. A general rule of thumb is to set aside 1-2% of the property's value each year for maintenance and repairs. However, this can vary depending on the age, condition, and type of property. Be sure to review and adjust your budget periodically based on actual expenses.

6. Educate Your Tenants

Your tenants play a significant role in the maintenance of your rental property. Well-informed tenants who understand their responsibilities can help prevent damage and alert you to any potential issues early on.

Start by including clear maintenance terms in your lease agreement. Define who is responsible for what—typically, tenants are responsible for keeping the property clean and reporting any problems, while landlords are responsible for repairing wear and tear and maintaining the property's systems and infrastructure.

Once a tenant moves in, provide them with a document that explains how to care for the property. This might include instructions on how to operate the heating and cooling systems, what to do in case of a plumbing issue, and reminders about tasks such as replacing smoke detector batteries and keeping outdoor areas tidy.

7. Plan for Major Upgrades

In addition to regular maintenance, rental properties will occasionally require more significant upgrades, such as a new roof, HVAC system, or appliances. These major expenses can take a big chunk out of your profits if not planned for.

Keep track of the age and condition of major systems and appliances in your property. Research their typical lifespan and plan for their eventual replacement. Setting aside a small amount each month in a separate savings account for these major expenses can make them more manageable when they do come up.

8. Embrace Technology

In today's digital age, technology can simplify property maintenance significantly. Property management software can automate many tasks, such as tracking maintenance requests, scheduling inspections, and even paying contractors. There are also many apps and platforms available to find and vet contractors, compare quotes for repair jobs, and more.

In summary, while property maintenance is an integral part of owning rental properties, it doesn't have to be a burden. By being proactive, organized, and strategic, you can maintain your properties with minimal effort and cost, ultimately enhancing the profitability of your real estate investment. In the next section, we'll dive deeper into how to manage rental properties efficiently, including finding and screening tenants, setting rental prices, and dealing with common landlord challenges.

Responsibilities of Landlords and Rights of Tenants

As a landlord, you have several responsibilities, and your tenants also have specific rights. Understanding these responsibilities and rights is crucial for maintaining a positive landlord-tenant relationship, avoiding legal issues, and ensuring your rental business runs smoothly.

1. Landlord Responsibilities

Landlord responsibilities can be categorized into legal, financial, and operational responsibilities. Let's dive into each category.

Legal Responsibilities

Federal, state, and local laws mainly govern your legal responsibilities as a landlord.

- **Housing and anti-discrimination laws**: The Fair Housing Act prohibits landlords from discriminating against tenants based on race, color, national origin, religion, sex, familial status, or disability. This applies to all stages of the landlord-tenant relationship, from advertising and tenant screening to evictions. Some state and local laws add additional protected classes, such as sexual orientation, marital status, and source of income.
- **Health and safety standards**: As a landlord, you must provide your tenants a safe and habitable living environment. This typically includes ensuring the property has proper heating, plumbing, electricity, and clean water, is structurally sound, and free from pests and hazards. Specific health and safety standards

can vary by state and local regulations.

- **Privacy laws**: Tenants have a right to quiet enjoyment of their rental property. This means landlords must provide notice before entering the property (except in emergencies) and cannot harass tenants or interfere with their use of the property.

Financial Responsibilities

Your financial responsibilities as a landlord primarily involve setting and collecting rent, handling security deposits, and managing property expenses.

- **Setting and collecting rent**: You have the right to set the rental price for your property (unless your property is rent-controlled). It's your responsibility to collect rent in a timely manner, provide receipts if requested, and handle any issues with late or unpaid rent.
- **Security deposits**: If you collect a security deposit from your tenants, you're usually required to return it at the end of the lease, minus any deductions for unpaid rent or damages beyond normal wear and tear. Many states have laws governing how security deposits are held

and returned.

- **Property expenses**: As the property owner, you're responsible for paying property-related expenses such as mortgage payments, property taxes, insurance, and maintenance costs.

Operational Responsibilities

Operational responsibilities refer to the day-to-day tasks of managing rental properties.

- **Maintenance and repairs**: As mentioned earlier, you must keep the property in good repair. This includes responding to maintenance requests, performing regular inspections, and maintaining the property's exterior and common areas.
- **Tenant relations**: Building good relationships with tenants can make property management easier and help prevent disputes. This involves communicating clearly and respectfully, promptly addressing tenant concerns, and fostering community in multi-unit properties.
-

2. Tenant Rights

Just as landlords have responsibilities, tenants also have rights. These rights serve to protect tenants from unfair treatment and ensure they have a safe and decent place to live.

- **Right to a habitable home**: Tenants have a right to live in a safe and habitable property. This means the property must meet basic health and safety standards, such as having working utilities, being free from pests, and having adequate heat and hot water.
- **Right to privacy**: Tenants have a right to quiet enjoyment of their rental property. Landlords must provide notice before entering the property (except in emergencies), and cannot harass tenants or interfere with their peaceful use of the property.
- **Right to fair treatment:** Under the Fair Housing Act and various state and local laws, tenants have a right to be treated fairly and not be discriminated against based on protected characteristics.
- **Right to security deposit return**: Unless there's a reason to make deductions (such as unpaid rent or

damages beyond normal wear and tear), tenants have a right to have their security deposit returned to them at the end of the lease.

Understanding your responsibilities as a landlord and your tenants' rights is essential for running a successful rental property business. Meeting your obligations and respecting your tenants' rights can create a positive rental experience, minimize disputes and legal issues, and contribute to a successful and profitable rental property investment. In the next section, we'll delve into how to find and screen potential tenants, set rental prices, handle lease agreements, and deal with common challenges that landlords face.

Growing Your Investments and Cashing In Your Equity

Building wealth in real estate involves more than just buying a property and collecting rent. It requires a strategic approach to growing your investments and leveraging the equity you've built. In this section, we'll delve into the strategies for expanding your portfolio, maximizing returns, and cashing in on your equity.

1. Understanding Equity and How It Grows

In real estate, equity refers to the difference between the market value of your property and the amount you owe on any mortgage. Equity can grow in two main ways: through appreciation (the increase in the property's value over time) and by paying down your mortgage.

Appreciation: Over time, real estate values generally increase due to factors like inflation, increased demand, and improvements in the local area. While appreciation isn't guaranteed and can vary widely based on location and market conditions, it can significantly boost your equity over the long term.

Mortgage paydown: Every time you make a mortgage payment, a portion goes towards reducing the principal amount of your loan. This increases your equity in the property. In the case of rental properties, your tenants essentially help you build equity by paying rent, which you then use to pay the mortgage.

2. Strategies for Growing Your Investments

Growing your real estate investments requires a strategic approach that aligns with your financial goals, risk tolerance, and management capabilities. Here are a few strategies to consider:

- **Buy and hold**: This strategy involves purchasing and holding onto a property for a long time to benefit from appreciation and rental income. It's a relatively passive investment strategy that can generate steady cash flow and significant wealth growth over time.
- **BRRRR (Buy, Rehab, Rent, Refinance, Repeat)**: This strategy involves buying a fixer-upper property, renovating it to add value, renting it out to generate income, then refinancing to recover the capital invested in the purchase and renovation. The recovered capital is then used to repeat the process with another property. The BRRRR strategy can accelerate portfolio growth, but it requires more work and expertise than the buy and hold strategy.
- **Value-add investments**: This strategy involves buying properties with potential for improvement, making those improvements, then raising the rents or selling the property at a higher price. This could involve anything from cosmetic updates to major renovations or adding new amenities. The goal is to increase the property's value and income potential.

- **Portfolio diversification**: Diversifying your portfolio can help mitigate risk and maximize returns. This might involve investing in different types of properties (e.g., single-family homes, multi-family properties, commercial properties), investing in different locations, or diversifying into other types of investments besides real estate.

3. Cashing In Your Equity

Equity is a form of wealth, but it's relatively illiquid—it doesn't put money in your pocket until you sell the property or tap into the equity. Here are a few ways to cash in your equity:

- **Sell the property**: If your property has appreciated significantly, selling it can unlock the equity you've built. However, selling comes with costs (like realtor commissions and capital gains taxes), and once you've sold, you'll no longer have the property to generate rental income.
- **Refinance**: Refinancing involves getting a new mortgage to replace your existing one. If your property has appreciated or you've paid down a

significant portion of your mortgage, you can often refinance for a higher amount and take the difference in cash. This allows you to access your equity without selling the property. The cash can be used to invest in more properties, make improvements, or for other purposes.

- **Home equity loan or line of credit (HELOC)**: These are loans that use your property's equity as collateral. They allow you to borrow against your equity and receive a lump sum (home equity loan) or a line of credit that you can draw from as needed (HELOC). These can be useful tools for accessing your equity, but they come with interest costs and the risk of foreclosure if you can't repay the loan.
- **Cash-out rent-back**: This relatively new strategy involves selling your property to an investor and then renting it back from them. This allows you to access your equity while continuing to live in or manage the property.

4. Leverage

Leverage is another powerful tool in growing your real

estate investments. In the context of real estate, leverage involves using borrowed capital to increase the potential return of an investment. In other words, you take on debt to buy a property, and if the return on the property exceeds the cost of debt, you make a profit.

For example, let's say you buy a property worth $100,000 with a down payment of $20,000 and a loan of $80,000. If the property appreciates by 5% in one year, it's now worth $105,000—a $5,000 gain. If you had paid cash for the property, your return would be 5% ($5,000 gain on a $100,000 investment). But since you only invested $20,000 of your own money, your cash-on-cash return is 25% ($5,000 gain on a $20,000 investment). That's the power of leverage.

Of course, leverage also increases risk—if the property's value goes down, or if you can't cover the mortgage payments, you could end up losing money. Therefore, it's crucial to use leverage wisely and consider factors such as interest rates, cash flow, and your risk tolerance.

5. Real Estate Partnerships and Syndications

If you're looking to grow your real estate investments but lack the capital or expertise to do it alone, forming a partnership or joining a real estate syndication can be a good option.

In a real estate partnership, two or more people pool their resources to invest in properties. Partnerships can be structured in many ways, but often, one partner provides the capital, while the other provides the expertise and does the work of finding, buying, and managing properties.

A real estate syndication is a group investment where several investors pool their money to invest in larger properties or projects that would be too expensive or complex for an individual investor. The syndication is usually managed by a sponsor or syndicator who oversees the investment and takes a share of the profits.

Partnerships and syndications can accelerate your investment growth by giving you access to more capital and expertise. However, they also involve shared control and potential conflicts, so it's important to carefully choose your partners or syndicators and have clear agreements in place.

6. Real Estate Investment Trusts (REITs) and Crowdfunding

Real Estate Investment Trusts (REITs) and crowdfunding

platforms offer another way to grow your real estate investments.

REITs are companies that own and operate income-producing real estate. They're traded on stock exchanges, so you can buy and sell shares just like stocks. This gives you a way to invest in real estate without having to buy properties directly, making it a more passive investment. REITs are required to distribute at least 90% of their taxable income to shareholders, so they can provide a steady stream of dividend income.

Real estate crowdfunding platforms allow you to invest in real estate deals online, often with a smaller amount of capital than would be required for direct property investment or REITs. Some platforms offer debt investments (you lend money for a property and earn interest), while others offer equity investments (you own a share of the property and earn a portion of the rental income and any appreciation).

While these options can help you diversify your portfolio and access larger deals, they also involve risks, such as lack of control, dependence on the management skills of others, and potential loss of capital. As always, do your due diligence before investing.

In the end, growing your investments and cashing in your equity in real estate isn't just about buying properties and waiting for them to appreciate. It's a strategic process that involves careful planning, smart financing, effective property management, and continuous learning. By understanding the various strategies and tools at your disposal, you can significantly enhance your wealth and create lasting financial success through real estate investing.

Chapter 7: Maximizing Your Rental Income

Strategies for Setting and Collecting Rent

The ability to generate a steady stream of rental income is one of the main appeals of real estate investing. Setting the right rent amount and ensuring efficient rent collection are two essential elements of maximizing your rental income. In this section, we will deep dive into the strategies that can help you set rent competitively and streamline your rent collection process.

1. Strategies for Setting Rent

The amount of rent you charge can make a significant difference to your rental income and return on investment. Here are some strategies to consider when setting rent:

Market Analysis

Before setting your rental rates, conduct a thorough market analysis. Look at similar rental properties in your area—properties with similar size, features, and location—and see what they're renting for. This will give you an idea of the going market rate. There are several online tools, like Zillow, Rentometer, and Craigslist, that you can use to research rental rates.

Remember, setting your rent too high can result in vacancies, while setting it too low can eat into your profits. Try to strike a balance where your property is competitively priced yet profitable.

Consider the Property's Amenities and Condition

When setting your rent, take into account your property's amenities and overall condition. A property with modern appliances, updated fixtures, a garage, or a yard can typically command a higher rent than a similar property without these features.

Additionally, the overall condition of the property can impact the amount of rent you can charge. If your property is older or has some cosmetic issues, you may not be able to charge as much as a similar but newer or more visually appealing property.

Understand Your Costs

Understanding your costs is crucial when setting your rent. Your costs will include your mortgage payment (if applicable), property taxes, insurance, maintenance and repair costs, and property management fees (if you use a property management company).

Your rental income needs to cover these costs, plus a margin for profit and unforeseen expenses. Make sure you're clear about what your costs are, so you know the minimum rent you need to charge to break even or make a profit.

Adjust for Market Changes

The rental market can and does change, so it's essential to

adjust your rental rates accordingly. If the demand for rentals in your area is high, you might be able to increase your rent. Conversely, if the market is saturated or demand is low, you might need to lower your rent or offer incentives to attract tenants.

Be aware of local regulations about rent increases, especially if your property is in a rent-controlled area. Some locations limit how much you can increase rent each year.

2. Strategies for Collecting Rent

Once you've set your rent, the next step is to collect it. Here are some strategies for efficient and effective rent collection:

Set Clear Payment Terms

Your lease agreement should clearly spell out the rental payment terms. This includes the amount of rent, when it's due, any grace period, late fees, and how the rent should be paid. Having clear payment terms can prevent misunderstandings and disputes.

Offer Convenient Payment Methods

The easier it is for tenants to pay their rent, the more likely they are to pay on time. Consider offering multiple payment methods, such as checks, bank transfers, or online payments through a property management software.

Online payments can be particularly convenient—they're quick, can be done from anywhere, and don't require you to handle physical checks. Many property management software options allow tenants to set up automatic payments, ensuring that the rent is paid on the same day each month.

Enforce Late Fees

Despite your best efforts, there may be times when a tenant pays their rent late. It's essential to have a policy in place for dealing with late payments, and this policy should be outlined in the lease agreement.

Typically, this involves charging a late fee if rent is not paid by a certain date. The fee should be enough to motivate tenants to pay on time but not so high as to be considered punitive or illegal. Remember to follow local regulations when setting and enforcing late fees.

Prompt Communication

If a tenant does not pay rent on time, communicate with them promptly. Send them a reminder of the missed payment and any late fees that apply. If they repeatedly pay late or miss payments, have a conversation with them to understand what's going on. They may be facing financial difficulties, or there may be an issue with the payment method.

Sometimes, you may need to work out a payment plan or take legal action to collect unpaid rent. However, it's usually best to try to resolve the issue through communication first.

3. Managing Vacancies

Vacancies can significantly impact your rental income, so it's crucial to minimize them as much as possible. Here are some strategies for managing vacancies:

Effective Marketing

To minimize vacancies, you need to attract tenants quickly. This starts with effective marketing. Your property listings should highlight the property's features and amenities, include quality photos, and provide all the necessary details about the property, rent, lease terms, etc.

Make sure to market your property in the right places. Online platforms like Zillow, Craigslist, Trulia, and social media platforms can be highly effective. If your property is in a college town, for instance, advertising on campus or in local student hangouts can be beneficial.

Competitive Pricing

Pricing your property correctly is crucial in minimizing vacancies. If your property is priced too high, you may struggle to find tenants. Conversely, if it's priced too low, you'll be leaving money on the table. Use market analysis to set a competitive price that attracts tenants while maximizing your income.

Early Renewal Incentives

Encouraging your current tenants to renew their leases can help avoid vacancies. Consider offering early renewal incentives, such as a small rent discount or an upgrade to the property, to encourage tenants to renew their lease.

Quick Turnaround Times

When a tenant moves out, aim to prepare the property for the next tenant as quickly as possible. This may involve cleaning, minor repairs, and possibly some improvements. The quicker you can get the property ready, the sooner you can start showing it to potential tenants.

4. Tenant Retention

Keeping your tenants longer can help minimize vacancies and the costs associated with finding new tenants. Here are some strategies for tenant retention:

Maintain the Property Well

Tenants are more likely to stay if they're happy with their living conditions. Regular maintenance and prompt repairs show tenants that you care about the property and their satisfaction.

Good Landlord-Tenant Relationship

Being respectful and responsive to your tenants can go a long way in retaining them. This means addressing their concerns promptly, keeping them informed about any changes or issues, and being considerate of their comfort and privacy.

Regular Rent Increases

While it's normal to increase rent periodically, large or frequent increases can drive tenants away. Try to keep rent increases reasonable and in line with the market. Be sure to give tenants adequate notice of any rent increases.

5. Rental Property Improvements

Improving your rental property can allow you to charge higher rent and attract and retain quality tenants. Some improvements that typically offer a good return on investment include:

Curb Appeal

Improvements to your property's exterior can make a strong first impression on potential tenants. This could involve landscaping, painting, or updating the front door or mailbox.

Kitchen and Bathroom Updates

Kitchens and bathrooms are often key selling points for rental properties. Updating them can significantly increase your property's appeal. This doesn't necessarily mean a full remodel; even small updates like new fixtures, a new backsplash, or updated cabinets can make a difference.

Energy Efficiency

Energy-efficient features can be a big draw for tenants and allow you to charge higher rent. Consider improvements like energy-efficient appliances, LED lighting, or improved insulation.

In conclusion, maximizing your rental income involves more than just setting and collecting rent. It also requires effective management of vacancies, good tenant relationships, and strategic property improvements. By employing these strategies, you can optimize your rental income and enhance the profitability of your real estate investment. In the next section, we'll delve into the strategies for developing a portfolio of rental properties, including the benefits of portfolio diversification, the use of leverage, and portfolio management tips.

Developing a Portfolio of Rental Properties

Expanding your real estate investments to include multiple rental properties can lead to more substantial income streams, more opportunities for appreciation, and better risk distribution. However, developing a portfolio of rental properties involves careful planning, diligent management, and strategic decisions. In this section, we will delve into the strategies and considerations involved in building a robust rental property portfolio.

1. Benefits of a Rental Property Portfolio

Before we explore how to develop a portfolio of rental properties, it's important to understand why you might want to consider this approach in the first place.

- **Increased Cash Flow**: More properties mean more rental income. While costs such as maintenance, insurance, and property management fees will also increase, rental properties tend to produce positive cash flow if they're well-chosen and well-managed.
- **Diversification**: Spreading investments across several properties can reduce risk. If one property is vacant or underperforming, the income from the other properties can help cover its costs. Also, owning properties in different locations or types of properties can protect you from fluctuations in local real estate markets.
- **More Opportunities for Appreciation**: The value of real estate tends to increase over time. By owning

multiple properties, you can benefit from appreciation across all of them.

- **Economies of Scale**: As you add more properties to your portfolio, certain aspects of property management can become more efficient and cost-effective. For instance, you might be able to negotiate better terms with contractors or property management companies.

2. Getting Started

If you're just starting in real estate investing, starting with one rental property is generally advisable. This allows you to learn the ropes of property management, understand the financial implications, and assess whether real estate investing fits you.

Once you've successfully managed one rental property and feel comfortable with the process, you can start considering adding more properties to your portfolio.

3. Financing Your Properties

Financing is often one of the biggest challenges when building a rental property portfolio. Here are a few ways to finance your properties:

- **Conventional Mortgages**: These are standard home loans banks and other lending institutions offer. They usually require a 20% down payment and have relatively stringent qualification requirements.
- **Government-Backed Loans**: Certain government programs, like the FHA loan or VA loan, offer more favorable terms, such as lower down payments or easier qualification. However, they often have restrictions, such as requiring you to live in the property for a certain period.
- **Home Equity Loans or Lines of Credit (HELOCs)**: If you have equity in your primary residence or another property, you can use a home equity loan or HELOC to finance a rental property.
- **Private Money or Hard Money Loans**: These are loans from private individuals or companies. They're usually more expensive than conventional loans, but they're more flexible and can be obtained quickly, which can be advantageous for certain deals.
- **Partnerships**: If you lack the capital to finance a property yourself, you might consider partnering with

someone else. They provide the capital, and you provide the real estate expertise.

Remember, leverage (using borrowed money to invest) can magnify your returns but also increase risk. Always consider your ability to cover the mortgage payments, even if the property is vacant or expenses are higher than expected.

4. Choosing the Right Properties

The success of your rental property portfolio largely depends on choosing the right properties. When evaluating potential properties, consider factors like:

- **Location**: Look for properties in areas with strong rental demand, good amenities, and potential for growth.
- **Cash Flow**: The property should produce positive cash flow—that is, the rental income should cover all the property's expenses and leave some profit.
- **Condition**: A property in need of significant repairs can eat into your profits. Unless you're specifically looking for a fixer-upper and you're confident you can

handle the repairs, look for properties in good condition.

- **Appreciation Potential**: While cash flow is crucial, appreciation can significantly boost your returns. Consider the property's potential for value growth.

5. Portfolio Management

Managing multiple properties involves more work and complexity than managing one. Here are some tips for effective portfolio management:

- **Stay Organized**: Keep clear records of income and expenses for each property. Use property management software to track rent payments, maintenance requests, lease documents, and other important information.
- **Outsource When Necessary**: If managing your properties becomes too time-consuming or stressful, consider hiring a property management company. They'll handle day-to-day management tasks for a fee, usually a percentage of the rental income.
- **Keep Up with Maintenance**: Regular maintenance can prevent costly repairs, keep your properties attractive

to tenants, and maintain their value.

- **Tenant Management**: Good tenant relationships can lead to longer tenancies and fewer issues. Communicate clearly, respond to issues promptly, and treat your tenants with respect.

Building a portfolio of rental properties can be a profitable venture, but it requires careful planning, strategic decision-making, and diligent management. Whether you're a new investor or looking to grow your investments, these strategies can help you build a robust rental property portfolio and enjoy the financial benefits of multiple rental income streams.

Generating a Thriving Rental Income

The ultimate aim of investing in rental properties is to generate a thriving rental income that not only covers all your costs but also provides a healthy profit. Achieving this requires a mix of strategies—from selecting the right properties and setting the right rent to managing properties and tenants effectively. This section will delve into how to put these strategies into action to maximize your rental income.

1. Strategic Property Selection

A thriving rental income begins with strategic property selection. This involves looking for properties that are likely to attract reliable tenants and provide a good return on investment.

Consider the property's location, its proximity to amenities, the local rental market, the property's condition, and its potential for appreciation. You should also consider the property's cash flow potential—after accounting for all costs, the rental income should leave a healthy margin.

2. Setting the Right Rent

Once you've selected a property, setting the right rent is crucial. If the rent is too high, you may struggle to find tenants, resulting in costly vacancies. If the rent is too low, you're not maximizing your income.

Research rents for comparable properties in the area to get an idea of the market rate. Also, consider your costs, the property's amenities, and the rental market conditions when setting the rent.

3. Effective Property Management

Effective property management is key to maximizing your rental income. This includes maintaining the property in good condition, addressing repairs promptly, and keeping the property occupied with reliable tenants.

Also, remember to periodically review your rents and adjust them as necessary to reflect changes in the market and the property's condition or amenities.

4. Good Tenant Management

A property is only as good as its tenants. Good tenants pay their rent on time, take care of the property, and are less likely to cause problems.

Screen your tenants carefully, checking their credit, employment, rental history, and references. Treat your tenants with respect, respond to their concerns promptly, and strive to maintain a good landlord-tenant relationship.

5. Regular Reviews and Adjustments

Your rental strategy should not be static—it should evolve with market changes, tenants, and properties.

Regularly review your rents, the condition of your properties, your property management practices, and the rental market. Be ready to adjust your strategies as necessary to maximize your rental income.

6. Ensuring Legal Compliance

Complying with all legal requirements is a matter of lawfulness and an important strategy to secure your income flow. Landlord-tenant laws regulate many aspects of the landlord-tenant relationship, including rent, security deposits, eviction procedures, and property condition. Violating these laws can result in fines, lawsuits, or other legal problems that can disrupt your rental income and harm your reputation.

Stay informed about the laws that apply to your rental properties. Depending on the property's location and your situation, this may involve local, state, or federal laws. When in doubt, consult with a knowledgeable real estate attorney.

7. Tax Planning and Efficiency

Understanding and planning for taxes can significantly

impact your rental income. Rental income is taxable, but landlords can deduct many expenses, including mortgage interest, property tax, insurance, maintenance costs, and depreciation.

Work with a tax professional who understands real estate investing. They can help you take full advantage of tax benefits, plan for tax payments, and avoid costly mistakes. Remember, good tax planning can significantly affect your net rental income.

8. Insurance Coverage

Adequate insurance coverage is a must for protecting your rental income. Insurance can cover the costs if a property is damaged or a tenant is injured. Without it, you could face large out-of-pocket expenses that eat into your rental income.

At a minimum, you should have property insurance that covers damage to the property and liability insurance that covers injuries or damage to others. Depending on the property and location, you may also need additional coverage, such as flood insurance or earthquake insurance.

9. Exit Strategy

Finally, it's important to have an exit strategy for each property in your portfolio. This strategy outlines when and how you will sell the property – whether to capitalize on appreciation, to cut losses, or to restructure your portfolio.

The exit strategy should take into account market conditions, property condition, capital gains taxes, and your overall investment goals. Having a clear exit strategy can help you maximize your profits when selling and protect your rental income during ownership.

In conclusion, generating a thriving rental income is about more than just collecting rent. It involves a comprehensive strategy that covers property selection, rent setting, tenant and property management, legal compliance, tax planning, insurance, and exit strategy. By carefully planning and managing each aspect, you can create a robust, reliable, and thriving rental income. In the final part of this book, we'll explore how to maintain a positive cash flow and analyze and compare rental investment properties to ensure long-term success in your real estate investment journey.

Chapter 8

Analyzing Your Investment

Tools and Metrics for Property Analysis

Understanding how to analyze potential investment properties is an essential skill for real estate investors. It's through this analysis that you can determine whether an investment opportunity will deliver the expected returns and align with your overall investment strategy. In this section, we'll explore the different tools and metrics you can use to perform this analysis and make more informed investment decisions.

1. Property Analysis Tools

Several tools can help you analyze potential investment properties. These tools typically involve some form of software or online platform that allows you to input various property details and then calculates key metrics. Some of the most popular property analysis tools include:

- **Spreadsheet Models**: Excel and other spreadsheet programs are common tools for property analysis. You can create a model that includes all the expenses, income, and key metrics you want to analyze.

- **Property Analysis Software**: Several real estate-specific software options provide more advanced analysis capabilities. These may include features for detailed expense tracking, loan amortization schedules, tax estimates, and more.
- **Online Platforms**: Many online real estate platforms, like Zillow or Redfin, provide some basic property analysis features. These can be a good starting point, especially for newer investors.

Remember, while these tools can be incredibly helpful, they're only as good as the data you put into them. Be sure to use accurate and comprehensive information when using these tools.

2. Key Metrics for Property Analysis

Several key metrics can help you evaluate potential investment properties. These metrics provide a snapshot of the property's financial performance and potential returns.

- **Gross Rental Yield**: This is a simple metric that shows the rental income as a percentage of the property's price. It's calculated by dividing the annual rental income by the property's price. For example, a property that costs $100,000 and generates $10,000 in annual rent would have a gross rental yield of 10%. This metric doesn't take into account any expenses, so it's a rough measure, but it's a useful starting point.

- **Net Rental Yield**: This metric improves on the gross rental yield by accounting for property expenses. It's calculated by subtracting annual expenses from the annual rental income, then dividing the result by the property's price. This gives a more accurate picture of the property's profitability.
- **Return on Investment (ROI)**: This metric shows the profit from an investment as a percentage of the amount invested. In the context of rental properties, ROI is typically calculated by dividing the annual net profit (rental income minus all expenses, including mortgage payments) by the total amount invested (including down payment, closing costs, and any repair or renovation costs).
- **Cash-on-Cash Return**: This metric is similar to ROI,

but instead of considering the total amount invested, it considers only the cash invested. This is particularly useful for properties bought with a mortgage, as it shows the return on the actual cash you invested.

- **Capitalization Rate (Cap Rate)**: This is a widely used metric in real estate investing. It's calculated by dividing the net operating income (rental income minus operating expenses, not including mortgage payments or other financing costs) by the property's price. The cap rate gives a snapshot of the property's profitability independent of your financing method.

3. Comprehensive Property Analysis

While these metrics can provide useful insights, it's important to remember that they're just part of the picture. A comprehensive property analysis should also consider factors like the property's condition and location, the local rental market, potential for appreciation, and your overall investment strategy.

For instance, a property with a high rental yield might seem attractive, but it might not be a good investment if it's in a location with high vacancy rates or low rental demand.

Similarly, a property with a low cap rate might still be a good investment if it's in a prime location with strong potential for appreciation.

4. Expense Estimation

Estimating expenses accurately is crucial for property analysis. Underestimating expenses can lead to a distorted view of potential returns and can cause unexpected cash flow problems. Typical rental property expenses include:

Mortgage payments: If you're financing the property, this will likely be your largest monthly expense.

Property taxes: These vary widely by location and are based on the property's assessed value.

Insurance: This covers potential damage to the property and liability risks.

Maintenance and repairs: These costs are inevitable and can vary significantly from year to year.

Property management fees: If you're using a property management company, these fees typically range from 8-12% of the monthly rent.

Vacancies: Budgeting for vacancies is wise, even in strong rental markets. A common rule of thumb is to assume a 5-10% vacancy rate.

Capital Expenditures (CapEx): These are major repairs or improvements that extend the life of the property, such as a new roof or HVAC system. It's important to set aside money each year for CapEx.

Utilities and services: Depending on your lease terms, you may be responsible for certain utilities or services, such as water, garbage collection, or landscaping.

Each expense should be estimated and included in your analysis as accurately as possible.

5. Financing Analysis

How you finance your rental property can significantly impact your returns. If you're using a mortgage, it's important to understand the terms of the loan and how they affect your cash flow and ROI.

The down payment, interest rate, loan term, and whether the loan is fixed or adjustable all play a role. Be sure to compare different financing options and consider getting pre-approved to better understand what you can afford.

6. Risk Evaluation

Every investment comes with risks, and real estate is no exception. When analyzing a potential property, consider the following risks:

- **Market risks**: Include changes in property values, rent levels, and vacancy rates. Research the local market and broader economic trends to assess these risks.
- **Property risks**: These include potential issues with the property itself, such as unexpected repair needs, problems with tenants, or changes in the neighborhood. A thorough property inspection and careful tenant screening can mitigate these risks.
- **Financial risks**: Include potential cash flow issues, interest rate increases (for adjustable loans), and unexpected expenses. Accurate expense estimation, conservative cash flow projections, and a solid financial buffer can help manage these risks.

Understanding and factoring these risks into your analysis can help you make more informed investment decisions and better prepare for potential challenges.

In conclusion, property analysis is a multi-faceted process that goes beyond simply looking at the purchase price and potential rental income. It involves a detailed examination of the property's expenses, potential risks, and financing options, as well as a consideration of the investor's own financial situation and investment goals. By conducting this comprehensive analysis, you can identify the best investment opportunities and maximize your returns.

Maintaining a Positive Cash Flow

Cash flow—the net income from a rental property after all expenses are paid—is the lifeblood of any real estate investment. Positive cash flow means your property is profitable, providing you with regular income and enhancing your financial security. However, maintaining positive cash flow isn't always straightforward—it requires strategic planning, careful management, and continual monitoring. Here, we will discuss strategies to maintain and improve the cash flow from your rental properties.

1. Accurate Rent Pricing

Your rental income is the most significant component of your cash flow. Therefore, setting the right rent price is crucial. If rent is too high, your property may sit vacant, leading to lost income. If it's too low, you could be missing out on potential income.

To set an accurate rent price, conduct a comparative market analysis. Look at what similar properties in the same area are renting for and consider factors such as the property's size, condition, amenities, and location. Remember to periodically review and adjust your rent prices to keep up with the market trends.

2. Minimize Vacancies

Vacancies can significantly impact your cash flow. Therefore, minimizing vacancies is key to maintaining positive cash flow. This includes:

- **Effective Marketing**: Good marketing attracts quality tenants faster. Highlight the property's selling points, use high-quality photos, and advertise on popular property listing websites.

- **Quick Turnarounds**: Once a tenant moves out, prepare and list the property as quickly as possible. This might involve cleaning, making minor repairs, or even making some upgrades.
- **Lease Renewals**: Keeping good tenants is often easier and more cost-effective than finding new ones. Provide an excellent renting experience, communicate effectively, and consider offering incentives for lease renewals.

3. Regular Maintenance and Timely Repairs

Regular maintenance and timely repairs keep your tenants happy and prevent minor issues from becoming major, costly problems. Inspect your properties regularly, address maintenance requests promptly, and budget for routine maintenance and unexpected repairs.

4. Careful Expense Management

Every dollar saved on expenses is a dollar added to your cash flow. Here are some ways to manage your expenses effectively:

- **Preventive Maintenance**: Regular maintenance can

prevent costly repairs down the line.

- **Energy Efficiency**: Energy-efficient appliances and fixtures can reduce utility costs if you're responsible for them.
- **Insurance and Tax Reviews**: Regularly review your insurance policies and property taxes to ensure you're not overpaying.
- **DIY Management**: If you have the time and skills, managing the property yourself can save on property management fees.

5. Robust Financial Planning

Having a solid financial plan helps ensure you can cover your expenses and still enjoy positive cash flow. This includes:

- **Budgeting**: A detailed budget helps you track income and expenses and plan for future costs.
- **Reserve Fund**: A reserve fund covers unexpected expenses or periods of vacancy without disrupting your cash flow.
- **Debt Management**: If you have a mortgage or other debt on the property, managing it effectively is crucial.

This might involve refinancing to a lower interest rate or making extra payments to reduce the principal.

6. Property Upgrades and Renovations

Improving your property can potentially allow you to charge higher rent and attract more tenants, thus increasing your rental income. However, it's important to focus on renovations that add value and appeal to renters. This could include upgrading the kitchen or bathroom, installing new flooring, painting, or adding a washer and dryer. Be sure to consider the costs and potential return on investment before embarking on any major renovations.

7. Tenant Retention

Retaining good tenants can save you the time and money involved in finding new ones, minimizing vacancies, and reducing potential wear and tear on the property. Provide excellent service, respond quickly to maintenance requests, and build positive relationships with your tenants. Regularly reviewing the terms of your lease and being willing to negotiate can also contribute to longer tenancies.

8. Effective and Efficient Property Management

Efficient property management is key to minimizing expenses and maximizing income. This might involve outsourcing certain tasks, like maintenance or rent collection, to free up your time for more strategic activities. If you have multiple properties, hiring a property management company might be cost-effective and can help ensure professional, consistent management.

9. Diversification

Owning rental properties in different locations can protect your cash flow from local market downturns or other location-specific risks. While managing properties in different locations can be more complex, it can also provide more stable, reliable cash flow.

10. Regular Cash Flow Analysis

Lastly, regular cash flow analysis is crucial. This involves regularly reviewing your income and expenses, tracking your cash flow, and comparing it to your projections. Regular analysis can help you identify issues early, monitor the effectiveness of your strategies, and make informed decisions to improve your cash flow.

In conclusion, maintaining a positive cash flow involves a combination of strategies that focus on maximizing income, minimizing expenses, and effectively managing your property and tenants. By implementing these strategies and regularly reviewing your cash flow, you can ensure your rental property provides a reliable, profitable income stream. In the next section, we'll delve deeper into how to analyze and compare different investment properties to select the ones that best fit your investment goals and risk tolerance.

Identifying a Good Return in Real Estate Investment

Investing in real estate is about more than simply buying property. It's about generating a good return on your investment. Identifying what constitutes a 'good' return in real estate investment is not a one-size-fits-all answer, as it depends on several factors, including your financial goals, risk tolerance, and the market conditions. However, understanding the various types of returns and the metrics used to measure them is key to making informed investment decisions. In this section, we'll delve deeper into these concepts and provide insights on how to identify a good return in real estate investment.

1. Types of Returns in Real Estate Investment

When investing in rental properties, there are typically two types of returns that investors seek: cash flow and appreciation.

- **Cash Flow**: This is the net income from a property after all expenses have been paid. It's the "income" part of the income-producing property. Positive cash flow means the property is generating a profit each month.
- **Appreciation**: This is the increase in the property's value over time. While cash flow can provide regular, monthly income, appreciation can result in a significant payoff when the property is sold.

Both cash flow and appreciation can provide a good return on investment, and many real estate investors aim to achieve a balance of both.

2. Measuring Returns: Key Metrics

Several key metrics can help measure the return on a real estate investment:

- **Return on Investment (ROI):** This metric considers both cash flow and appreciation. It's calculated by dividing the net profit (annual cash flow plus appreciation) by the total amount invested.
- **Cash-on-Cash Return**: This metric shows the return on the actual cash invested in the property, making it especially useful for properties purchased with a mortgage.
- **Capitalization Rate (Cap Rate)**: This is the ratio of a property's net operating income to its purchase price, providing a useful measure of a property's profitability.
- **Internal Rate of Return (IRR)**: This sophisticated metric considers both the timing and the amount of cash flows, providing a comprehensive measure of an investment's profitability over time.

Each of these metrics provides a different perspective on the return, and investors typically look at several of them to get a full picture of a property's potential return.

3. Factors Influencing Returns

Several factors can influence the returns on a real estate

investment, including:

- **Property Factors**: The condition, location, and type of property can influence both cash flow and appreciation.
- **Market Conditions**: Real estate markets can fluctuate based on factors such as the economy, interest rates, and supply and demand dynamics.
- **Management**: Effective property management can maximize rental income, minimize expenses, and maintain property value, all of which contribute to a good return.
- **Financing**: The terms of any loans used to purchase the property will influence the return.

Understanding these factors can help you identify properties that are likely to provide a good return.

4. What is a 'Good' Return?

What constitutes a 'good' return can vary depending on several factors:

- **Investment Goals**: If your goal is to generate immediate income, you might prioritize properties that offer strong cash flow. If you're more interested in long-term wealth building, you might focus more on appreciation potential.

- **Risk Tolerance**: Higher returns often come with higher risk. If you're more risk-averse, you might be satisfied with a lower, but more reliable, return.
- **Market Averages**: Understanding the average returns in the market can provide a benchmark to assess potential investments.

5. Appreciation Potential

While cash flow is a vital part of investing in rental properties, it's also important to consider a property's potential for appreciation. The potential for a property's value to increase over time can significantly boost your return on investment.

To evaluate a property's appreciation potential, you'll need to consider factors like:

- **Location**: Properties in desirable neighborhoods or in areas with strong economic growth often have higher appreciation potential.

- **Market Trends**: Understanding local and national real estate trends can help predict future appreciation.
- **Property Condition**: Properties that are in good condition or have been recently renovated might appreciate more quickly than those in need of significant repairs.

6. Cash Flow Analysis

Analyzing cash flow is an essential step in identifying a good return on a real estate investment. This involves examining all income and expenses associated with the property.

Key elements to consider in a cash flow analysis include:

- **Rental Income**: This is the main source of income for rental properties. It's important to research local rental rates to ensure you're setting a competitive rate for your property.
- **Operating Expenses**: This includes property taxes, insurance, maintenance and repairs, management fees, and any utilities or services you'll be paying.
- **Vacancy and Bad Debt**: It's a good practice to factor in

a certain percentage of the rental income for potential vacancies and non-payment.

- **Financing Costs**: If you're using a mortgage to finance the property, you'll need to include the monthly loan payment in your expenses.

By subtracting the total expenses from the total income, you can determine the net cash flow. Positive net cash flow indicates that the property is generating a profit, while negative cash flow indicates a loss.

7. Risk Assessment

Identifying a good return on a real estate investment isn't just about calculating potential income—it's also about considering the risks. The higher the risk, the higher the return should be to compensate.

To assess risk, you should consider factors such as:

- **Market Stability**: Markets with stable economies and steady population growth tend to be lower risk than those with volatile economies or declining populations.
- **Tenant Quality**: Properties that attract high-quality

tenants tend to be lower risk than those that attract unreliable or problematic tenants.

- **Property Condition**: A property in good condition is usually less risky than one that requires significant repairs or maintenance.

Understanding the risk associated with an investment property can help you determine if the potential return is worth the risk.

In conclusion, identifying a good return in a real estate investment requires a comprehensive understanding of the various aspects of real estate investing. It involves careful analysis of potential income, thorough assessment of risks, and sound knowledge of your personal investment goals and risk tolerance. By mastering these areas, you can make more informed investment decisions and boost your chances of achieving a good return on your real estate investments. In this book's next and final chapter, we will wrap up everything we've discussed and provide a roadmap to take you from being a beginner investor to a successful real estate mogul.

Chapter 9

Overcoming Challenges

Common Pitfalls in Low-Cost Property Investments and How to Avoid Them

While the prospect of investing in low-cost properties can be alluring, it's important to acknowledge that this route can come with its unique set of challenges. These hurdles can range from finding and financing properties, to dealing with maintenance and tenant issues. However, these obstacles can be navigated successfully with careful planning, due diligence, and proactive management. In this final chapter, we'll dive deep into the common pitfalls you may encounter when investing in low-cost properties and provide you with strategies on how to avoid them.

1. Underestimating the Total Cost of Ownership

One common pitfall novice investors fall into is underestimating the total cost of owning a rental property. While the low purchase price of an investment property may seem like a bargain, it's essential to factor in all the other costs associated with owning and maintaining the property. These may include costs for repairs and renovations, property taxes, insurance, property management, and potential vacancy periods.

To avoid this pitfall, perform a comprehensive cost analysis before purchasing a property. Use conservative estimates and ensure you have sufficient funds or access to financing to cover all potential costs. In the case of older properties, a thorough home inspection is crucial to identify any underlying issues that could lead to significant expenses down the line.

2. Overlooking Property Location

Another common mistake is failing to consider the importance of location. Finding low-cost properties in less desirable neighborhoods or areas with high vacancy rates or low rental demand is possible. However, a property in a poor location can lead to longer vacancy periods, lower rents, and less tenant interest.

To avoid this pitfall, research the location thoroughly before investing. Look at factors such as local amenities, crime rates, schools, and employment opportunities. Speak to local real estate agents, property managers, and even residents to better understand the area.

3. Neglecting Tenant Screening

The quality of your tenants can make or break your rental property investment. Problematic tenants can lead to unpaid rents, property damage, and legal issues, all of which can eat into your profits.

To avoid this pitfall, implement a thorough tenant screening process. This should include checking prospective tenants' credit scores, rental history, employment status, and personal references. A well-defined leasing agreement is also crucial to set clear expectations and protect your rights as a landlord.

4. Inadequate Property Management

Managing a rental property involves more than just collecting rent. It includes responsibilities such as regular property maintenance, dealing with tenant issues, and complying with landlord-tenant laws. Inadequate property management can lead to tenant dissatisfaction, property damage, legal issues, and financial loss.

To avoid this pitfall, consider hiring a professional property management company, particularly if you own multiple properties or live far from your rental property. Although this involves additional cost, it could save you money in the long run by ensuring that your property is well-maintained, tenanted, and compliant with legal requirements.

5. Inadequate Financing Strategy

While low-cost properties are more affordable, they may not always qualify for traditional financing options. Inadequate or improper financing can lead to financial stress and could risk repossessing your property if you can't keep up with mortgage payments.

To avoid this pitfall, carefully consider your financing options before purchasing a property. Speak with a financial advisor or a mortgage broker who understands real estate investing. Exploring various financing options such as bank loans, private loans, or seller financing can give you a broader view of what's available and what fits your investment strategy best.

6. Failure to Plan for the Unexpected

As with any investment, real estate comes with risks. Market fluctuations, unexpected expenses, problematic tenants, or periods of vacancy can all impact your cash flow and overall return.

To avoid this pitfall, always have a contingency plan. Set aside a reserve fund to cover unexpected expenses or periods of vacancy. Regularly review your insurance coverage to ensure you're adequately protected. Diversify your investment portfolio to spread risk and provide stability even if one investment underperforms.

7. Ignoring Local Laws and Regulations

One often overlooked pitfall in low-cost property investments is ignoring local laws and regulations related to owning and managing rental properties. These can include local zoning laws, landlord-tenant laws, property standards bylaws, and local licensing requirements. Ignorance or non-compliance with these laws and regulations can result in costly fines, legal disputes, and even eviction proceedings.

Avoid this pitfall by familiarizing yourself with all relevant laws and regulations before purchasing a property. Seek legal advice if needed and ensure that all your actions as a landlord are legally compliant. This also extends to understanding the tax implications of owning a rental property. Enlist the help of a qualified accountant who can help you navigate tax deductions, capital gains, and other related financial matters.

8. Falling for "Too Good to be True" Deals

While low-cost properties can indeed be profitable, investors must beware of deals that seem "too good to be true". In their eagerness to grab a bargain, some investors may overlook significant issues such as major structural problems, problematic locations, or unresolved legal disputes. These issues can lead to massive unexpected costs that can turn a seemingly great deal into a financial nightmare.

To avoid this pitfall, always perform due diligence before purchasing a property. This includes thoroughly inspecting the property, reviewing all legal documents, and researching the local area. If a deal seems too good to be true, it probably is. Listen to your instincts and don't be afraid to walk away if something doesn't feel right.

9. Not Factoring in the Cost of Time

Real estate investment, particularly low-cost property investment, can be time-consuming. Between property maintenance, tenant management, paperwork, and dealing with unforeseen issues, the time commitment can be significant. Underestimating the time investment can lead to stress and even burnout, which can affect the overall profitability and enjoyment of your investment journey.

Avoid this pitfall by factoring in the time cost when considering an investment opportunity. If you have limited time, consider investing with partners or hiring a property management company. Remember, time is a valuable resource and should be factored into your overall return on investment calculation.

10. Neglecting Long-Term Strategy

Successful real estate investment is not just about buying a property and collecting rent. It's about having a clear, long-term strategy. Without a strategic plan, investors can get caught up in the day-to-day operations and lose sight of their long-term goals and exit strategy. This lack of direction can lead to poor decisions and missed opportunities.

Avoid this pitfall by having a clear plan and investment

strategy from the outset. This includes having clear financial goals, understanding your risk tolerance, and having a predefined exit strategy. Regularly review and update your plan as necessary and make decisions that align with your long-term goals.

In conclusion, while low-cost real estate investment offers many exciting opportunities, it is not without its challenges. However, by understanding the potential pitfalls and adopting strategies to avoid them, you can navigate your investment journey with confidence and success. The key is to stay informed, make calculated decisions, and always keep your long-term goals in mind. Real estate investing is not a get-rich-quick scheme, but with patience, diligence, and smart strategies, it can be a rewarding path to financial freedom. As you apply the insights from this book and continue to learn and grow, you'll be well on your way to building a profitable real estate portfolio.

Case Studies of Overcoming Challenges

Every real estate investment journey is unique, filled with its share of successes and challenges. Understanding how others have navigated their challenges can provide valuable insights and practical strategies that you can apply in your journey. In this section, we'll explore three case studies of real estate investors who encountered and successfully overcame challenges in their low-cost property investments.

Case Study 1: From Underestimation to Comprehensive Planning

John, a first-time investor, was attracted by the low purchase price of a rental property in an up-and-coming neighborhood. He bought the property intending to generate positive cash flow from the rent, but he quickly found himself facing mounting expenses. He had underestimated the renovation costs and the time it would take to get the property rent-ready. Additionally, he hadn't factored in the property management costs and the time commitment needed to manage the property and tenants.

Faced with these challenges, John decided to pause and reevaluate his approach. He sought help from a mentor and started educating himself about the various aspects of real estate investment. He learned about comprehensive cost analysis and understood the importance of considering all potential costs before purchasing a property.

John also realized that his time was valuable, and he needed help managing the property. He decided to hire a property management company, which freed up his time and ensured that the property and tenants were professionally managed.

Today, John owns several rental properties and credits his initial challenges for teaching him the importance of comprehensive planning and the value of professional property management. His experience highlights the importance of thorough cost analysis, the value of education and mentorship, and the role of property management in successful real estate investing.

Case Study 2: From Problematic Tenants to Thorough Tenant Screening

Sarah, an experienced real estate investor, had always had good luck with her tenants. However, when she purchased a low-cost property in a different neighborhood, she faced a series of problematic tenants who were consistently late on rent, caused property damage, and were disruptive to the neighbors. These issues resulted in costly repairs, legal issues, and stress for Sarah.

Recognizing that she needed a better way to select tenants, Sarah implemented a thorough tenant screening process. She started checking prospective tenants' credit scores, rental history, employment status, and personal references. She also sought legal advice and implemented a well-defined leasing agreement to set clear expectations and protect her rights as a landlord.

Implementing these strategies has made a significant difference for Sarah. She now attracts higher-quality tenants who respect the property and pay their rent on time. Her experience underscores the importance of thorough tenant screening and a clear leasing agreement in managing rental properties.

Case Study 3: From Overleveraging to Strategic Financing

David, an ambitious real estate investor, was eager to grow his portfolio quickly. He leveraged his properties to the hilt to purchase more properties. However, when the real estate market took a downturn, and some of his properties sat vacant for longer than expected, he struggled to keep up with his mortgage payments.

Facing the risk of foreclosure, David had to sell some properties at a loss to reduce his debt. This experience was a wake-up call for David. He realized he had taken on too much debt too quickly without considering the potential risks.

David took a step back to reevaluate his financing strategy. He started consulting with a financial advisor before making new investments. He learned about various financing options and started diversifying his financing methods to reduce his risk. He also learned about the importance of having a reserve fund to cover unexpected expenses or periods of vacancy.

Today, David's real estate portfolio is thriving, and he's more cautious about taking on debt. His experience serves as a reminder of the risks of overleveraging and the importance of strategic financing in real estate investing.

Case Study 4: From Poor Location Choices to Data-Driven Decisions

Amy, a novice real estate investor, was excited to find a low-cost property that seemed like a steal. She quickly snapped it up, hoping to reap high rental returns. However, she found it challenging to attract and retain tenants due to the property's location in a high-crime, low-amenity neighborhood. The low rental income and high tenant turnover ate into her profits and left her feeling frustrated and disillusioned.

Recognizing her mistake, Amy began to take a more strategic approach to property selection. She started researching neighborhoods extensively, considering factors such as crime rates, amenities, schools, and economic growth. She used data from local real estate websites, government reports, and neighborhood forums to gain a holistic view of potential locations.

Amy's new approach paid off. Her next investment was a property in a neighborhood with a strong rental market, and it quickly attracted long-term tenants. Her experience shows the importance of thorough location analysis and the value of data-driven decision-making in real estate investing.

Case Study 5: From Unexpected Expenses to Building a Contingency Fund

Jake, a seasoned real estate investor, bought a low-cost property with a seemingly healthy cash flow. However, he was hit with several unexpected expenses, including a major roof repair and a prolonged vacancy period. These expenses severely impacted his cash flow and put financial stress on Jake.

This experience taught Jake the importance of being prepared for the unexpected. He began setting aside a percentage of his rental income into a contingency fund. This fund acted as a safety net, covering unexpected expenses without disrupting his cash flow or requiring him to dig into his personal savings.

Today, Jake continues to grow his portfolio of low-cost properties, confident in the knowledge that he is prepared to handle unexpected expenses. His experience emphasizes the importance of a contingency fund in managing rental properties.

Case Study 6: From Short-Term Focus to Long-Term Planning

Laura, an eager investor, started her investment journey with a short-term focus. She looked for properties that would give her quick returns, often neglecting long-term factors such as property quality, location, and appreciation potential. This short-sighted approach led her to make impulsive investment decisions that didn't pay off in the long run.

Facing a stagnating portfolio, Laura decided to shift her focus. She started analyzing each potential investment with a long-term perspective, considering not only immediate returns but also the property's potential for long-term growth and appreciation.

This shift in focus led Laura to make more calculated investment decisions. Her properties not only provided immediate rental income but also appreciated over time, contributing to her overall wealth. Laura's journey illustrates the importance of long-term planning in real estate investing.

In closing, these additional case studies serve to further underscore the main challenges that investors may face when dealing with low-cost property investments. They offer practical lessons learned from real-world situations, providing you with tested strategies that can help you avoid common pitfalls in your investment journey. These tales of overcoming challenges should inspire you to approach your investment journey with a sense of preparedness, resilience, and a long-term perspective. They show that with a well-informed strategy, you can turn obstacles into opportunities and pave your way to a successful and profitable real estate investment career. Here's to your upcoming successes in the fascinating world of real estate investing!

Navigating Market Changes

Real estate investing is intrinsically linked to market changes, and understanding how to navigate these changes is vital to the success of your investments. In this section, we'll explore what market changes entail, their potential impacts on low-cost property investments, and strategies to navigate them effectively.

1. Understanding Market Changes

Market changes refer to shifts in the real estate market influenced by a variety of factors, including economic conditions, interest rates, demographic trends, and government policies, among others. These changes can affect property values, rental demand, and investor sentiment. For instance, economic downturns can lead to decreased demand for rental properties, while population growth in a certain area can drive up rental prices and property values.

2. Impacts on Low-Cost Property Investments

Market changes can significantly impact low-cost property investments. For example, an economic downturn might result in lower rental demand, making it harder to find tenants or forcing you to lower your rental rates. On the other hand, positive changes such as neighborhood revitalization or improved local amenities can increase the desirability of your property and boost its value.

Market changes can also affect the financing of low-cost properties. Interest rates, in particular, play a significant role. Higher interest rates can increase your mortgage payments and decrease your cash flow, while lower interest rates can make it cheaper to finance properties.

3. Strategies for Navigating Market Changes

Navigating market changes can be challenging, especially for novice investors. However, several strategies can help you manage these changes effectively.

Stay Informed: Knowledge is power when it comes to

navigating market changes. Stay updated on real estate trends and news. Attend seminars, read real estate blogs and books, listen to podcasts, and join real estate investment groups. The more informed you are, the better equipped you'll be to navigate market changes.

Diversify: Diversification can help buffer against market changes. This could mean diversifying within real estate - owning properties in different neighborhoods, cities, or even types of properties. You could also diversify outside of real estate, such as in stocks or bonds. Diversification can provide a level of protection against market volatility.

Long-Term Perspective: Real estate should be viewed as a long-term investment. While market changes can impact short-term profitability, the long-term trend for real estate has historically been upward. Don't be overly concerned about short-term market changes. Focus on properties that will be profitable in the long run.

Build a Cash Reserve: A cash reserve can help you weather market changes. This could be used to cover mortgage payments if you have a vacant property or unexpected maintenance issues. A good rule of thumb is to have at least three to six months' worth of expenses in a reserve fund.

Adjust Strategy as Needed: While having a clear investment strategy is important, it's also crucial to be flexible and adjust your strategy in response to market changes. This might mean shifting from a strategy focused on capital growth to one focused on cash flow, or vice versa, depending on market conditions.

In conclusion, while market changes are inevitable, they do not have to derail your investment goals. With careful planning, informed decisions, and strategic actions, you can navigate these changes and continue on your path to investment success.

4. Building Relationships in the Real Estate Industry

One of the most effective ways to navigate market changes is by fostering strong relationships within the real estate industry. These relationships can offer invaluable insights, support, and opportunities, helping you make more informed investment decisions.

Realtors can provide current market data and industry trends, lenders can offer flexible financing options during market fluctuations, and experienced investors can share insights and advice based on their experiences with similar market changes. Moreover, building relationships with contractors, property managers, and real estate attorneys can ensure you have a reliable team to support your investment operations.

To build these relationships, consider joining local real estate investment clubs or online forums. Attend industry events, participate in webinars, or even consider finding a mentor who can guide you through your investment journey. Always be genuine in your interactions and seek win-win outcomes to cultivate long-term, mutually beneficial relationships.

5. Capitalizing on Market Changes

While market changes can pose challenges, they can also present unique opportunities for savvy investors. For example, during an economic downturn, property prices may drop, creating a buyers' market where investors can acquire properties at lower costs. On the other hand, a booming economy might result in increased rental demand, allowing property owners to raise rents and improve their cash flow.

To capitalize on these opportunities, it's crucial to stay informed and be ready to act quickly when the right opportunity presents itself. This might mean having your finances in order, knowing your investment criteria, and being willing to make decisions quickly.

Additionally, consider adopting investment strategies that can thrive in different market conditions. For instance, a buy-and-hold strategy can be advantageous in a rising market, where property values are increasing, while a rental strategy can provide consistent cash flow in a flat or declining market.

6. Resilience and Persistence in the Face of Market Changes

Lastly, successful navigation of market changes requires a level of resilience and persistence. Market changes can be unpredictable and can test an investor's resolve. However, it's important to remember that market downturns are typically followed by recoveries, and short-term market fluctuations should not derail your long-term investment goals.

When faced with challenging market changes, remain focused on your long-term objectives, stay adaptable, and continue to make informed decisions based on your investment strategy and risk tolerance. Real estate investing is not a smooth, straight path, but a journey with ups and downs. Those who persist and continue to learn and adapt are the ones who will ultimately succeed.

To wrap up, while navigating market changes can be complex, the strategies outlined here will provide a robust framework for managing these fluctuations. By staying informed, building strong industry relationships, capitalizing on opportunities, and staying resilient, you can turn market changes into stepping stones rather than stumbling blocks on your real estate investment journey.

As this book concludes, remember that the journey of real estate investing is a marathon, not a sprint. It requires patience, knowledge, and a willingness to learn and adapt. With the insights and strategies you've gleaned from this book, you're well-equipped to start your journey on a strong footing, navigate the challenges ahead, and steer your path to success. So, as you step into the world of real estate investing, do so with confidence, ambition, and the knowledge that you have the tools and strategies to succeed. Thank you for reading, and here's to your success in the exciting world of real estate investing!

Conclusion

Achieving Financial Freedom Through Real Estate Investing

As we reach the end of this comprehensive guide to real estate investing, it's time to bring all the pieces together and look at the big picture: achieving financial freedom. We've explored the many aspects of investing in low-cost properties, from understanding the real estate market and preparing financially, to finding and financing properties, and navigating market changes. Now let's focus on the ultimate goal that makes the journey worthwhile - financial freedom.

1. Understanding Financial Freedom

Financial freedom means having enough income to pay for living expenses for the rest of your life without having to work full time. Some people achieve financial freedom through savings and investments, while others build a business that generates passive income.

In the context of real estate investing, financial freedom is achieved when the income generated from your properties - after all expenses have been deducted - is enough to cover your living expenses. This allows you to live the life you desire without worrying about financial constraints.

2. Real Estate Investing as a Path to Financial Freedom

Real estate investing, especially in low-cost properties, presents an accessible and realistic path to financial freedom for many people. Unlike other investment vehicles, real estate offers multiple income streams, including cash flow, appreciation, and tax benefits.

Rental properties, in particular, provide a steady cash flow in the form of rental income. This is a passive income stream, meaning it requires little to no work on your part once the property is rented out. Over time, as you acquire more properties, this rental income can add up to a substantial amount, contributing significantly to your financial freedom.

3. Building a Profitable Portfolio

The key to achieving financial freedom through real estate investing is building a profitable portfolio of properties. This involves buying properties at a good price, in a good location, and with a good potential for return. It requires thorough analysis, strategic financing, and good property management.

Remember, the goal is not just to own properties, but to own profitable properties. This means properties that generate more income than they cost in mortgage payments, maintenance, taxes, and other expenses. Your profit is what contributes to your financial freedom.

4. Persistence and Patience

Achieving financial freedom through real estate investing is not a get-rich-quick scheme. It requires persistence, patience, and a long-term view. It involves overcoming challenges, learning from mistakes, and constantly adapting to changing market conditions.

But with each challenge overcome, you become a more skilled and knowledgeable investor. With each property acquired, you move one step closer to your goal of financial freedom. And with each mistake made, you gain valuable lessons that contribute to your growth and success as an investor.

5. The Reward of Financial Freedom

The journey to financial freedom through real estate investing may be challenging and filled with uncertainties, but the reward is well worth it. Financial freedom offers more than just monetary wealth. It provides the freedom to live life on your own terms, to pursue your passions, and to spend time with your loved ones. It offers the security of knowing you're financially prepared for whatever life throws your way. And it provides the satisfaction of knowing you've achieved your financial goals through your hard work, dedication, and savvy investing.

6. Continuous Learning and Adaptation

Achieving financial freedom through real estate investing is not a one-time event but a continuous journey. The real estate market is dynamic, with new trends, regulations, and opportunities constantly emerging. Successful investors are those who stay informed and adapt their strategies based on these changes.

Commit to continuous learning by reading books, attending seminars, joining real estate investment clubs, and networking with other investors. Make it a point to stay updated on market trends, interest rates, and investment strategies. As you gain experience and knowledge, refine your investment approach and diversify your portfolio to mitigate risk and maximize returns.

7. The Role of Professional Advisors

As you build your portfolio and wealth, consider seeking the guidance of professional advisors. Accountants, financial planners, and real estate attorneys can provide valuable advice on tax strategies, estate planning, and legal considerations. While there's a cost associated with their services, the peace of mind and potential savings can be well worth it.

8. Giving Back

Financial freedom is not just about accumulating wealth but also about making a positive impact. Many successful real estate investors choose to give back to their communities by contributing to affordable housing initiatives, mentoring aspiring investors, or supporting local businesses. As you achieve your financial goals, consider how you can use your success to make a difference.

9. Enjoying the Journey

Finally, it's important to enjoy the journey towards financial freedom. Celebrate your achievements, learn from your setbacks, and take pride in your progress. Real estate investing can be challenging, but it can also be rewarding and exciting. Embrace the journey with optimism, resilience, and a sense of adventure.

As you move forward on your path to financial freedom, remember the power of real estate investing. With the right knowledge, strategy, and mindset, you can transform low-cost properties into a source of passive income, financial security, and lasting wealth. This book has provided you with the tools and insights to start this journey. The next steps are up to you.

Encouragement for Future Real Estate Investors

Now that we have traversed the extensive path of real estate investing, let's take a moment to reflect on the journey ahead for you as a future real estate investor. This final section aims to leave you with words of encouragement, inspiration, and the much-needed motivation to propel you forward in your real estate investment journey.

1. Embrace the Journey:

Firstly, remember that real estate investing is not merely a transaction or a one-time event but a journey. And like all journeys, it is filled with moments of success and challenge, excitement and anxiety, learning and growth. Embrace this journey with an open mind and a resilient spirit. Celebrate your achievements, learn from your challenges, and know that each step, no matter how small, brings you closer to your goal of financial freedom.

2. Stay Informed and Be Adaptable:

The world of real estate is dynamic and ever-evolving. It rewards those who stay informed and adaptable. Continually educate yourself about the market trends, new policies, emerging opportunities, and innovative strategies. Be ready to adapt your approach based on these insights. Remember, flexibility is a significant asset in the world of real estate investing.

3. Cultivate Patience and Persistence:

Success in real estate investing doesn't happen overnight. It requires patience, persistence, and a long-term perspective. It might take months, if not years, to find the right property, secure financing, or attain profitable returns. Stay patient, stay persistent, and stay focused on your goals. Your persistence will pay off in the end.

4. Make Data-Driven Decisions:

In real estate investing, your decisions should be driven by data, not emotions. Always conduct thorough research and analysis before making any investment decision. Use the tools, metrics, and strategies discussed in this book to guide your decisions. Remember, an informed investor is a successful investor.

5. Leverage the Power of Community:

You are not alone in your real estate investment journey. There is a vibrant community of real estate investors who can offer support, advice, and camaraderie. Join local real estate investment clubs, participate in online forums, attend industry events, and connect with fellow investors. The insights and relationships you gain from this community can be invaluable.

6. Believe in Your Potential:

Finally, and most importantly, believe in your potential. Real estate investing is not reserved for the wealthy or the privileged. It is an accessible path to financial freedom for anyone who is willing to learn, work hard, and persevere. No matter your background, education, or experience, you have the potential to succeed in real estate investing. Believe in this potential, harness it, and use it to fuel your journey to financial freedom.

In closing, this book has equipped you with the knowledge, strategies, and insights to embark on your real estate investment journey. But the true power lies within you - your determination, your resilience, your ambition. With these qualities, you can navigate the path of real estate investing, overcome the challenges, seize the opportunities, and achieve your financial dreams.

So, as you stand on the precipice of your real estate investing journey, remember these words of encouragement. Take the leap, embrace the journey, and never stop believing in your potential. You are more powerful than you think, and you have the capacity to achieve remarkable success.

Thank you once again for reading this book, and for allowing us to be a part of your exciting journey. We wish you all the best in your real estate investing endeavors. Here's to your success, your financial freedom, and the extraordinary journey that lies ahead!

In the immortal words of Ralph Waldo Emerson: "Do not follow where the path may lead. Go instead where there is no path and leave a trail." You're about to carve your unique path in the world of real estate investing. Have faith in yourself, be brave, and remember, every great journey begins with a single step. This is your first step. Treasure it, cherish it, and make the most out of it.

Go forth, future real estate investor. The world of real estate investing awaits you. Good luck, and here's to your success!

Appendix

Glossary of Key Terms

1. **Appreciation**: The increase in the value of a property over time due to factors like market inflation, increased demand, and improvements made to the property.

2. **Cash Flow**: The net income from a rental property after mortgage payments and operating expenses have been made. A positive cash flow means the property is generating a profit.

3. **Equity**: The difference between the market value of a property and the outstanding amount on any loans secured by the property.

4. **Gross Yield**: A property's annual rental income as a percentage of its purchase price.

5. **Leverage**: Using borrowed money to finance an investment. In real estate, this often refers to using a mortgage to purchase a property.

6. **Net Yield**: Gross yield minus any operating costs (like maintenance, property management fees, and insurance),

expressed as a percentage of the property's purchase price.

7. **Return on Investment (ROI)**: A measure of the profitability of an investment. In real estate, this is typically calculated as the annual return from a property (rental income and appreciation) divided by the total investment in the property.

8. **Tenant**: A person who pays rent to live in a property owned by someone else.

9. **Vacancy Rate**: The percentage of all available units in a rental property that are vacant or unoccupied at a particular time.

Useful Resources for Further Reading

1. "**The Book on Rental Property Investing: How to Create Wealth With Intelligent Buy and Hold Real Estate Investing**" by **Brandon Turner**: Provides practical advice on building wealth through rental properties.

2. "**Rich Dad Poor Dad**" by **Robert Kiyosaki**: A classic personal finance book that emphasizes the importance of investing, including real estate investing, for wealth creation.

3. "**The Millionaire Real Estate Investor**" by **Gary Keller**: Offers insights into successful investment strategies and wealth-building habits from over 100 millionaire investors.

4. **BiggerPockets**: An online community of real estate investors with forums, blogs, and podcasts that offer a wealth of information and insights on real estate investing.

5. **Zillow**: A real estate and rental marketplace that provides data on home prices, rental rates, and local real estate markets.

6. **LoopNet**: A leading mobile and online real estate marketplace that connects tenants and investors with opportunities.

7. **Realtor.com**: Provides listings for homes for sale and for rent, along with mortgage tools and real estate news.

8. **Meetup**: Allows you to find and join local real estate investment clubs where you can network with other investors.

9. "**The ABCs of Real Estate Investing: The Secrets of Finding Hidden Profits Most Investors Miss**" by **Ken McElroy**:

Provides insights into successful strategies for finding and managing investment properties.

This collection of terms and resources should provide a useful foundation for your ongoing real estate investment journey. Remember, continued learning and growth are critical components of success in real estate investing. As you continue to build your knowledge and expertise, these resources and others will be invaluable tools in your investment toolkit. Best of luck as you embark on this exciting path to financial freedom!

Table of Contents

Investing in Rental Properties 2
for Beginners..... 2
Introduction..... 4
Chapter 1..... 8
Understanding Real Estate Investing..... 8
Chapter 2..... 16
Low-Cost Real Estate: The Untapped Goldmine..... 16
Chapter 3..... 27
Preparing to Invest: Financial Planning..... 27
Chapter 4..... 39
Finding and Financing Your Property..... 39
Chapter 5..... 51
The Buying Process..... 51
Chapter 6..... 69
Owning and Managing Properties..... 69
Chapter 7: Maximizing Your Rental Income..... 88
Chapter 8..... 109
Analyzing Your Investment..... 109
Chapter 9..... 130
Overcoming Challenges..... 130
Conclusion..... 152
Appendix..... 161
Glossary of Key Terms..... 161
Useful Resources for Further Reading..... 163

www.ingramcontent.com/pod-product-compliance
Lightning Source LLC
LaVergne TN
LVHW011632200926
848484LV00010B/2537